GAME PLAN

Leadership Lessons
from the Best of the NFL

KENDALL GAMMON

Game Plan: Leadership Lessons from the NFL
Copyright © 2008 by Kendall Gammon

It's A SNAP Inc.
14429 Maple Street
Overland Park, Kansas 66223

ISBN 13: 978-0-9815574-1-0
ISBN 10: 0-9815574-1-4

Printed in the United States

www.kendallgammon.com

Cover and Book Design by Gwyn Kennedy Snider

DEDICATION

To Tommy Allen Riggs.
You led at all levels of your life. Your vision helped others realize their potential. Your belief and guidance made what seemed unrealistic to some, a reality to all. You performed at a level higher than your age required. The memory of you continues to drive me in my daily life. You were my brother-in-law, but more importantly, you were my friend.

I miss you each and every day.

ACKNOWLEDGEMENTS

I would like to thank the following coaches and players for their help with *Game Plan*: Dick Vermeil, Jack Del Rio, Bobby April, Trent Green, Morten Andersen, Tony Richardson, Mike Vrabel, Kevin Greene, Kevin Mawae and Danny Weurffle.

In addition, thank you to Dr. Caron Goode and Amy Collins for their help and understanding with this project during some of the most difficult circumstances I have been through in my life.

Finally, thank you to my wife Leslie and two boys, Blaise and Drake, for their unconditional love that is a true blessing in my life.

TABLE OF CONTENTS

INTRODUCTION

Winning is never accidental.
All successful coaches and payers…
have at least one thing in common:
a strong game plan.

Lou Holz

Football professionals hold unique secrets of leadership that apply to life. Exceptional leaders, including the ones I've had the privilege of playing with, respond to extraordinary circumstances with a well-defined plan; a critical path to success. Brute, physical strength gets players down the field, but it is the character of the man or woman in the game that defines their ability to rise to leadership.

What differentiates people who always seem to come out on top and those who don't? I believe one inherent quality is their positive outlook, a combination of optimism and positive thinking, which I discussed in my first book, *Life's a Snap* (It's a Snap, Inc. 2005). However, there is so much more.

The leadership lessons in this book come from some of my favorite NFL coaches and friends. You'll find that winners handle themselves differently, internally and externally. *GAME PLAN* will show you how to:

- Mentally prepare for success
- Relate to others
- Present yourself
- Match words with actions every time
- Conquer adversity

Leadership is a choice. Once a person makes that momentous choice, they gain the respect of others and become stars in their own right. Choosing leadership takes a player far beyond the field, into the real world where they are as successful as they choose to be. This book defines the character of a leader and provides the steps for becoming a successful leader. The ability is within you.

Winning is success, and you choose to win as well as to succeed. I encourage you to choose to live on your own terms, rather than have terms dictated for you. There are no limits to your dreams or achievements when you make a conscious decision about how you are going to live and what you want to accomplish.

Within the NFL world, we learn to build a team, participate as a team member, and watch how other leaders build their teams. The team is akin to our family, tribe, community, or business group. Each of us belongs to a team at some level, and more likely we belong to several groups that offer us opportunities to learn leadership. The skills of the leadership game are the skills for life.

The contributors to this book are my team. We believe that, as leaders, we have a responsibility to give back to our communities. Here's my lineup.

MORTEN ANDERSEN

Andersen is the all-time leading scorer in the NFL despite being the oldest player in the NFL. He experienced the most accurate season of his career in 2006-07 as the kicker for the Atlanta Falcons. His physical skills, accuracy, and gamesmanship are only a few of his leadership traits, which shone when he was a member of the Saints, then the Falcons, Giants, Chiefs and Vikings. His career highlights include being selected to play in the Pro Bowl seven times and holding multiple NFL records including most games played (382), and most field goals (585). He also has the distinction of being the highest scoring player in Pro Bowl games with forty-five points.

The stats don't tell the whole story, however. Morten is a natural born leader who has taken his skill set and honed it to the "highest level," as he would put it. He is truly a chameleon. His ability to get along with anyone and everyone is something to be studied and emulated. In my time with him, it was easy to see why he not only survived, but flourished in the NFL. I think his ability to "recognize the moment" and what it demands, is a trait I saw and tried to emulate. He is constantly aware of what his surroundings require at any given moment, and he responds accordingly. The NFL is filled with pressure, certainly for kickers in game-winning moments, but he's been able to separate from the pressure, responding when necessary, and relaxing when able. I've seen others who ultimately could not handle such pressure in similar situations, and pressured themselves out of the league. Morten and I spent only two years together, but as the two eldest members of the Chiefs at the time, we had much in common and stay in touch to this day. We became part of each other's "inner circle."

BOBBY APRIL

A special teams coordinator for the Buffalo Bills, Bobby honed his coaching skills in university arenas for Tulane, the University of Arizona, University of Southern California, and Ohio State. His leadership skills show in his relationships with his team members reflected by their improved performances and stats.

April's opportunity to train with excellence continued in the NFL when he first became special teams coach with the Falcons. His career has also included stops with the Steelers, Saints, and Rams. In 2004, April became the special teams coordinator for the Buffalo Bills. He also holds the title of assistant head coach. It is an elite group of special teams coaches that are assistant head coaches as well. This certainly validates the importance of Bobby's contributions to the team.

Personally, I credit Bobby for pushing me to the highest level as a long snapper in the NFL. He was brutally honest at times, which is what my career called for at that point. Bobby is one of the more dynamic leaders I've been around in my life. His ability to communicate in an effective, concise manner is second to none. His reputation as a teacher and motivator of players is to be admired.

JACK DEL RIO

Currently head coach for the Jacksonville Jaguars, Jack has always been a versatile athlete with superb physical skills and mental strength. His professional football career started as a third round draft pick in 1985 for the New Orleans Saints. He then moved to the Kansas City Chiefs, Dallas Cowboys, and then the Minnesota Vikings, and played in the Pro Bowl in 1994.

The Miami Dolphins signed Del Rio for the 1996 season, but he was released before opening day. Del Rio decided it was a good time to retire as a player and contemplate his next move, which turned out to be his coaching career. Del Rio signed on as the strength and conditioning coach for the Saints, then moved to the position of linebacker's coach for the Ravens. As defensive coordinator for the Panthers, Del Rio built and led one of the toughest defensive units in the NFL.

In 2003, following his pattern of excellent leadership, Del Rio became the second head coach of the NFL's Jacksonville Jaguars. One thing that always struck me about Jack was that he had a goal, and a game plan to get there. In a conversation we had while working out in the New Orleans Saints weight room, Jack talked of his dream to be a head coach in the NFL, and his proposed timeline. His plan was ambitious, to say the least. It took him 20 percent longer to reach that goal of becoming a head coach, but I would guess it to be 50 percent less time than many other head coaches took to accomplish the same goal.

The one thing that was always true of Jack, and still is to this day, is that he has a plan and a time frame to get there. This, along with his personable skills that you will learn from in this book, make him special—not only as a coach, but as a human being.

KEVIN GREENE

This leader's skills were evident at Auburn University when he won an award for Defensive Player of the Year in 1984. He earned a degree in criminal justice and moved on to the L.A. Rams as a fifth round draft pick in 1985. Greene became known for his sacks record, second in the league that year, which positioned him for a continued challenge to maintain his record. He did, and was selected for the All-Pro team in 1989. In 1993, Greene moved from the Rams to the Steelers, maintained his top status in the defensive realms, which earned him three consecutive Pro Bowls as well as in Super Bowl XXX.

Next, Greene helped take the then new team, the Carolina Panthers, to their NFC Champion Game. The year 1996 proved to be golden for Greene. His superb display of strength, skill, and leadership for his team captured these prestigious awards: NFC Linebacker of the Year, NEA Defensive Player of the Year, NFL Linebacker of the Year. He led the NFL in sacks and once again went to the Pro Bowl. He moved to the 49ers for one year and back to the Panthers for two more years. He achieved his fifth Pro Bowl in 1998, and retired with a record of 160 sacks by a linebacker. In his fifteen-year career, Greene played 228 games and six conference championships.

TRENT GREEN

Trent is the "personable" quarterback, a leader among his teammates and two-time quarterback in the Pro-Bowl. He started his professional career in 1993 as a draft choice of the San Diego Chargers. In his career, Green has thrown for over 4,000 yards in multiple seasons as he moved from the Chargers to the Canadian Football League's British Columbia Lions, to the Redskins, then the Rams, the Chiefs, and finally the Miami Dolphins. Green's career includes a Super Bowl XXXIV championship while with the St. Louis Rams and he was a two-time recipient of the Derrick Thomas Most Valuable Player award while with the Kansas City Chiefs.

I refer to Trent as the "finest human being I know." He truly sets the standard, not only as a football player and teammate, but also as a father, husband, friend, and man of faith. He has endured some of the worst experiences you can imagine, not only in football, but personally as well. Still, he maintains the role of charismatic leader.

KEN KEIS, MBA, CPC

Keis is the non-sports player in this book, and a fine sportsman, nonetheless. He pays several roles—dad and family man, internationally known author, speaker and consultant, and CEO.

In the past twenty years, he has conducted more than 2,000 presentations, including 10,000 hours of coaching and HR consulting. He has published 300 articles, and designed more than 40 business management, leadership, personal development, wellness, or sales processes—writing more than 2 million words of content along the way. His new book assists others in discovering their purpose: *My Source Experience Journal–A Personal Discovery Process for Those Who Want to Lead a Passionate and Fulfilling Life.*

Keis is president and CEO of Consulting Resource Group International, Inc., founded in 1979. Many professionals herald CRG as the number one global resource center for personal and professional development.

A certified professional consultant with an MBA in international management, Keis is considered one of the foremost global experts on how assessment strategies and processes not only increase, but actually multiply success rates. Called "one of the most passionate presenters you will ever experience," Keis is also an Internet radio host, popular television and radio guest, and seminar speaker. His mission is sharing CRG's unique developmental models to assist individuals, families, teams, and organizations to realize their potential and purpose in the emotional, mental, psychological, intellectual, interpersonal, physical, financial, and spiritual areas of life.

KEVIN MAWAE

Mawae was inducted into the LSU Athletic Hall of Fame in 2007. He was selected to the Pro Bowl six consecutive times as a result of his athletic prowess as a center in the NFL. He was with the Seahawks for three seasons, the Jets for seven, and has been with the Tennessee Titans since 2006.

As a center, Kevin is responsible for making offensive line calls quickly and decisively during the game. His success or failure means the QB will either be able to sit back safely in the pocket and distribute the ball to playmakers, or get sacked by the other team.

The tenacious way in which he plays the game is in stark contrast to the quieter, controlled personality off the field. Kevin is a devoted father, husband, and friend. People have confidence in Kevin and the values he holds dear. This is most evident, football-wise, in the fact that he is a longstanding member of the NFLPA executive committee, voted in by the players themselves. This elite ten-member board is asked to represent the nearly 2,000 players of the NFL.

TONY RICHARDSON

This leader was born in Germany and spent his first eight years there before moving to the United States. A three-sport letterman while living in Daleville, Alabama, Tony attended Auburn University and started most of his four seasons there as a fullback.

His career continued as an undrafted free agent with the Dallas Cowboys in 1994, where he spent most of the time on the practice squad before being released. He signed with the Kansas City Chiefs in the subsequent off-season.

While in Kansas City, Richardson became a pillar of not only the team, but also the community. He is noted for blocking for Hall of Famer Marcus Allen when he scored his one hundredth touchdown. Later, he became a star in his own right as he paved the way for Priest Holmes and his record-setting seasons. For these accomplishments, he was voted to the Pro Bowl in 2003, 2004, and 2005.

As a free agent after the 2005 season, Tony moved on to the Minnesota Vikings and continued a successful career, having been selected to the Pro Bowl in 2008 for helping lead the way for the up-and-coming star running back Adrian Peterson.

Personally, Tony is a great friend who I have relied upon for many years. His passion for football, and for life in general, is apparent in everything he does. Tony is more generous with his personal time than anyone I know. He realized long ago that the NFL stage he is on allows him to influence people of all walks of life.

Like Kevin Mawae, he is a member of the NFLPA's ten-member executive committee, and for good reason. His strength as a communicator is evident from the moment you meet him. Tony is never complete, always seeking to grow. He is always striving to become a better, more well-rounded person. Additionally, he is the only player I know who attained his Master's degree while playing the demanding game that is football in the NFL.

DICK VERMEIL

With one Super Bowl Championship under his belt, Vermeil retired as head coach of the Kansas City Chiefs in 2006 after an exemplary career. Vermeil coached the Philadelphia Eagles from 1976 through 1982. During that time, he was named NFL's Coach of the Year and took the Eagles into Super Bowl XV. While those were great accolades with which to retire from NFL coaching, Vermeil then returned in 1997 to coach the St. Louis Rams. The season's successes were few. With experience, time, and new players, Vermeil and the Rams won Super Bowl XXXIV over the Tennessee Titans. Earning the title of NFL Coach of the Year in 1999, Vermeil again "retired," only to sign on later with the Kansas City Chiefs. Currently, Vermeil is a game analyst for college football broadcasts and for NFL games.

Coach Vermeil is very unique because he openly recognizes faults within his team and within himself. He speaks his mind, which is something I don't believe enough people do in this day and age. While I think he would admit that sometimes it has not served him well, overall it endeared him to the thousands of men he has led over his illustrious career. Dick has a very deep appreciation for what a person can do for the team and for him, but more importantly, each person can do for the ultimate in self-development. He often talks of instilling confidence in people to help them be the best they can be, not just as football players, but as human beings. Vermeil's interest has returned huge dividends professionally. It's my belief, however, that he has taken much more satisfaction in witnessing people's personal growth than in any trophy he's ever hoisted above his head.

MIKE VRABEL

Michael Arace, sports reporter for *The Dispatch* of Columbus, Ohio, calls Vrabel reliable: "Vrabel's numbers are adding up. He has 542 tackles, 371 solo, and 44 sacks in seven seasons with the Patriots. These figures speak to consistent production of the highest level." (02-03-08)

Mike Vrabel played for the Pittsburgh Steelers from 1997 through the 2000 season. He then moved to the New England Patriots to become a major cog in the Patriots' defensive unit. Vrabel played in Super Bowl XXXVI, and was a contender for Super Bowl MVP in XXXVIII. He also played in Super Bowl XXXIX, where he caught a two-yard touchdown pass.

It wasn't until Super Bowl XLII that he actually experienced a Super Bowl loss after a much-celebrated 16-0 perfect regular season. Vrabel was selected for the Pro Bowl in 2007 as a starter, and in January 2008, was named to the All-Pro team.

Mike is a football player who is passionate for the game. I truly believe he would play for free. It's this love for the game, I think, that ultimately endears him to his teammates. He sets the bar high.

DANNY WUERFFEL

Winning the Heisman Trophy as a quarterback at the University of Florida started Wuerffel's NFL career. He is the only Heisman Trophy recipient to receive the "Draddy," an award which is presented by the National Football Foundation and the College Football Hall of Fame to the nation's top football scholar-athlete.

Drafted by the New Orleans Saints in 1997, Danny played three years, including one year with the Rhein Fire of the NFL's European League and was the MVP in World Bowl 2000.

Wuerffel returned to the U.S. NFL and played one season each for the Green Bay Packers, Chicago Bears, and Washington Redskins. He then retired from the NFL to participate in another calling—what he felt was his true calling—to work in New Orleans with Desire Street Ministries, a faith-based, non-profit organization. An inspirational speaker, Danny invigorates and empowers everyone around him. His strong faith in God is evident in everything he does. Some have a hard time with people who wear their faith on their sleeve. In Danny's case, however, people of strong, wavering, or even little, faith are drawn to him. He has an aura about him that breaks down all walls. He is truly an amazing person and someone who I was able to turn to time and again while we were teammates in New Orleans.

OUR HOPES

The world needs leaders as well as followers. Inherently, we are both. I wrote this book with the intention that you become not only a better leader and teammate, but also a better person. My hope is that you are able to assimilate many of the techniques throughout the book for your personal growth and professional leadership development.

As I recount stories and lessons from our days in the NFL, you will see that it is not only possible to succeed in a high stress environment like the National Football League, but also to flourish and have fun.

You will learn the secrets that many successful coaches and players have used to succeed in the NFL games, and ultimately the game of life. The NFL stands for National Football League, but many also refer to it as "Not For Long," referring to the fact that the average player's career is less than four years. The typical rate, and the head coaches' expectations, of success is three years or less. This book will tell you how they have not only lasted in the "Not For Long" league, but enjoyed themselves as well.

I would encourage you to take notes, highlight and generally deface this book in any way that will help you remember the skills needed to make your success a reality.

In the NFL, if you lose a playbook, you can be fined more than $1,500. It's my belief that you risk far more by not incorporating the thoughts and ideas contained within these pages. This is your playbook to leadership, team building, and success. This is your Game Plan.

CHAPTER ONE

Trailblazers on the Field

You are never really playing an opponent.
You are playing yourself, your own highest standards,
and when you reach your limit,
that is real joy.

Arthur Ashe

At certain points in their lives, some young men said "yes" when challenged or invited to stretch beyond their comfort zones. That "yes" set in motion the learning process of acquiring leadership skills of excellence. When you learn their personal stories and discover the decisions they've made along the way, you'll observe their characters forming. You'll see whom they admired as teammates and who inspired their leadership as they've motivated me. This chapter is about making the decisions that grow into leadership skills.

Do you remember the precise moment in your life when a coach, parent, or teacher put their full faith in your ability to accomplish a task? Their faith in you was so unwavering, resolute and steadfast, that your stomach heaved and your knees buckled? That person you respected invited you to cross the line from fear to confidence and step up to the task.

Because they believed in you, you swallowed your fear and stepped over the line. When you stepped over the line, you chose leadership.

I chose leadership when I was a fifteen-year-old freshman in high school. The head coach, Lloyd Liby, asked me to consider playing at the varsity level. He felt that my skills were enough to play against boys who would be four years older than me. I accepted and was a starter two games into the season.

By the end of the year, I had become a leader, not because of what I said, but because I said little and simply respected those above me and those older than me. My leadership skills were in my actions—how I practiced and played. I competed intensely and my love of the game showed. I had stepped over that line as a fifteen-year-old boy. I chose leadership, and with it came an awesome feeling of confidence.

Morten Andersen stepped into a moment of leadership with the legendary quarterback Kenny "the Snake" Stabler.

Morten:

"In 1983, my locker was next to his in the Saints locker room, and I often saw him walk the talk. We were playing the Atlanta Falcons in the old Fulton County Stadium, and we were down by two points and had less than two minutes to go. We were moving the football, and I had a thirty-five yarder from the left hash to win the game. It was a beautiful afternoon out there.

"Kenny 'The Snake' Stabler, an outstanding high school athlete, received contract offers from several pro teams. However, he chose to play college football at the University of Alabama. He then moved on to the NFL and played for the Oakland Raiders and, with his team, won the 1976 Super Bowl Championship. Late in his career, Kenny moved on to the Oilers and finally the Saints.

"I was so nervous that I was sweating bullets. I was coming on to the field and Kenny was standing with the referee, arm draped over the ref's shoulder (something only a veteran like Kenny could do), letting the clock run down. When the clock hits three seconds, he called timeout. Now, I'm going out for one of my first game wins as an NFL player against our nemesis and archrival, the Atlanta Falcons. So as Kenny was coming off the field, I was going on to the field.

"'Morton let's go home!'

"Those words caught me completely off guard. He could have said how much we needed this kick in the last three seconds of the game.

"He could see the fear in me; my eyes were as big as tea cups. Well, he grabbed me firmly on the shoulder,

3

then grabbed my arm, and looked right at me with a smirk on his face. He said, 'Morton let's go home.'

"He had to know how nervous I was, but his calmness suddenly calmed me. I went out and kicked it, and we did go home.

"He pushed me to step over the line. It takes a leader to recognize these high-pressure situations and totally deflate them. I learned a lot from him on how to handle these big situations with humor and with quiet confidence."

WHAT IS A GREAT LEADER?

A leader commands respect, and the best way to command respect is to be somebody who does things the right way every time.

A great leader will exhibit character consistently, regardless of whether anybody's watching.

One of the keys in being able to lead is to show people that you're willing to do it yourself first. Show that willingness to serve, and others are willing to follow.

A great leader recognizes the needs of the situation and adjusts to the personality he is leading, whether it is a grizzled veteran, a seasoned master, or a rookie kicker destined for the NFL Hall of Fame.

MOMENT OF VISION

For a high school athlete of exceptional ability, the visit or phone call from a scout seeking talent for the pros inspires a cascade of mental images. Those pictures could include running down the field making the one-handed impossible catch in mid-air or perhaps kicking the winning field goal. It might even be making the snap for a game-winning field goal. Every good player started with a vision of his future greatness, and every good leader evolved into the greatness of this vision.

Kevin Mawae, selected for six consecutive Pro Bowls, is a leader among men. He is a persistent and durable player and succeeded in playing an unbroken streak of 177 games until an arm injury took him out of the game in October 2005. First, his skills make him a leader at the top of his game, followed by his valuable experience and time in the league. I asked him what qualities he sees in himself that draw people to him.

Mawae:

"Some of us are blessed with more ability than others, but I think the guy that takes ability and hones it, makes it better than it already was to automatically attract others. I think that guy earns a great deal more respect in the locker room than somebody who's naturally gifted but never works at it.

"My longevity in the game definitely helps because

the longer you're in the game, the more people pay attention.

"I'm also approachable, and I like to be approached. I enjoy meeting other people and opening myself up to them. When you have that kind of charisma, then naturally people will listen."

In addition to a positive self-perception, Kevin feels that leaders need to be straight shooters. "Leaders cannot dance around issues," Kevin says. "Otherwise, people will approach that leader with skepticism, doubt, and questions such as: *Can I trust him? Is he telling me the truth? What is he hiding? Why is he avoiding the issue?*"

Morten Andersen's view of a leader's self-perception suggests that humor helps a leader not take the game too seriously.

Andersen:

"How seriously do you take yourself? I mean let's look at the big picture. I'm playing a kid's game here. This is a very privileged existence that we've carved out for ourselves because we get paid very well to play a game we love. So how seriously can you take yourself? My brother still claims I haven't worked a day in my life! I'm the luckiest human being alive here.

"Also I would say that Clay Matthews is the single most influential leader I know who truly lived his vision of leadership—one of the top three players that I've ever played with. As a linebacker who played for nineteen

years with the Cleveland Browns, he was remarkable
to be able to play that position so long, be in the kind
of shape that he was, and take the physical abuse that
he did."

Clay Matthews hails from a family of pro ball
talent. His father and brother were NFL players
and his three sons play at the college level. The
Cleveland Browns drafted Matthews from USC, and
he played nineteen seasons in the NFL with both
the Cleveland Browns and the Atlanta Falcons.

Moreover, the way he handled himself off the
field and in relationships was such an inspiration to
me. He was a leader by doing. He was an intelligent
man, an intelligent player, and everything I wanted
to be as far as a professional—a good family guy, a
good ball player and teammate. He knew that to be
around this league, he'd have to constantly work
on his skills. Clay Matthews had no false sense of
entitlement, and that's why he played as long as he
did.

Jack Del Rio, coach of the Jacksonville Jaguars,
started his coaching career in the NFL as an assistant
strength coach while I was with the New Orleans
Saints. Jack was actually paying more for his kids
to go to school than he was making as the assistant
strength coach in New Orleans. Jack has always been
a man who does what is necessary to achieve his
goals. He also helped coach linebackers. He later
became the linebackers' coach for the Baltimore

Ravens. Del Rio was then hired as defensive coordinator of the Carolina Panthers in 2002 before being named to his current position in January 2003. However, leadership training started for this veteran when the New Orleans Saints made him their third round choice in the 1985 draft.

From 1981 through 1984, as a linebacker for the University of Southern California, Jack practiced and played hard. Team players competed each day and hounded each other with friendly jibes to do their best. He practiced and played for New Orleans the same way, pushing to the end. Yet, some team members said to him several times, "Hey rookie, slow down, man. What are you trying to prove?"

As Jack explains,

Del Rio:

"I fell into the practice of not competing the way I should. And it showed, as our team wasn't good then. That kind of thinking, 'slow down...' can be detrimental to you as it was for me. I had to choose to go all the way. For a football team or the leadership to have that slow-down kind of mentality pulls in the wrong direction.

"Of the successful team's programs I have been with I've watched these attitudes be phased out: the climate of anti-work, the attitude of us versus them, and the mentality of player versus coach."

Dick Vermeil was a bored high school student who had no ambition to go to college. He would have been content to work in his dad's garage. However, his high school coach said, "You can do better. Go to college... You could be a coach too." Vermeil credits his first coach with planting the seed for this ambition, and each time he needed more encouragement, another bright light inspired him forward to leadership.

Vermeil emulated the leadership traits of his early influences as he refined his personal coaching style, which garners respect. Vermeil describes leadership this way:

Vermeil:

"Your leadership role after a win is different than a leadership role after a loss. Leadership starts over every day, I think. It starts over every year with a new football team. It starts again after every game.

"Leadership is a beacon that guides you every day. Today we won, so how would a leader react? Today we lost, how would a leader react? Responses to winning and losing would be different, and how a leader communicates that response is consistent with his everyday character because a leader:

- makes people realize that they are capable of so much more. People may not realize their potential at first until they are poked or prodded into stretching beyond limitations.

- No matter how many members, a leader puts a team together to raise the capacity and energy of the whole group.

- A leader's job is to help people use their talents and to do so unselfishly by respecting their responsibilities and holding them accountable.

"Now, I've always believed that from high school coaching, on up the ladder, relationship building helps you gain insight into how you can help an individual if there are some holes like lack of confidence or understanding. A leader has to have insight about their team members. You can't help or communicate appropriately if you don't have any real understanding of what a person is like, what motivates him, what's holding him back, what's prevented him from being all he can be. That's why I always took that leadership approach.

"Plus, I've always enjoyed that part of the intense competition because it made it all the more worthwhile when you bond with your organization. You bond with your coaching staff, your players, and everybody in the organization is of utmost importance. I've been around situations in which the only people that were treated real well are the top dollar people. Well, to me, I didn't believe in that approach."

I agree with Coach Vermeil that relationship building is based on your genuine interest in people's lives outside of football. Each of us plays different roles on different teams. A leader's role is to sharpen and stretch the team member to greatness. So it's a win-win situation. Improving little deficiencies, which we all have, helps that person become a better player who can then make a greater contribution to the team.

Any man, whether a husband, father, corporate executive, coach or player, displays true leadership with these five traits, according to Vermeil. I asked him which top five traits he attributes to himself that he consciously models for others.

Vermeil:

1. "I've always felt I had a very good feeling, or awareness, of another person and what was on his mind.

2. "I knew how to help him even though he may not even recognize his faults. So, I've always felt that a guy couldn't bullshit me because I could read it. I could read how sincere he is about his career, his relationships and his teammates. I could tell whether they were selfishly motivated or if they were sincere.

3. "I always felt that I understood the process of what it takes to win, and I've always felt a lot of people complicated it. But it isn't that complicated. I had the opportunity to demonstrate it in high school, junior college, college, and pro-football with three different pro-teams. By the third year in all three pro-football teams, we won seventy-three percent of our games, and all three of them were in the playoffs, where they hadn't been. One of them won the world championship. In our third year in Kansas City, we were thirteen and three.

4. "I had the patience and the discipline to stick with it and not be swayed or distracted by the naysayers. Every organization has the second-guessers, who serve to look over your shoulder. You've got to realize that's the way it is in the world.

5. "Then I think the fifth trait is persistence. I've always had a lot of energy. One of the reasons I left the Chiefs after the five years, is I sensed I was running out of energy. I felt that position required somebody with tremendous stamina, and at seventy years old you're not what you were at sixty years old; that's all there is to it."

CHOOSING TO ACT AS A LEADER

Bobby April, assistant head coach, special teams for the Buffalo Bills, is in a unique leadership position to shape and encourage the talents for special teams players. April explains, "This position requires that I be personal and enthusiastic with each team member. My passion for the role is contagious, and a leader creates an infectious passion through the natural desires to help people be better, and eventually do their best."

Leadership, in April's eyes is action, not a position. In the game of football, a coach asks players to exert energy and effort in addition to taking risks. Sounds like most organizations, yet the risks may vary. What skills do leaders demonstrate that enables a player to follow their lead and be willing to take risks? April believes the following traits belong to every leader.

April:

"**Knowledge** of the game or the business has to be high, and the leader has to be creative in using his knowledge. Knowledge in your field makes you credible, but how you use that knowledge is the backbone of leading, an action work. A leader is a continuous learner who keeps abreast of the content in his field, but also he learns from his life experiences that shape him for better or for worse.

"**Intuition** in leadership is how you handle people and situations, often following a perception or gut-level feeling instead of logic.

"**Learning** helps a leader respond to creative conversations. A leader who values learning will understand different dynamics in motivating a player, child, or a colleague—and be on the cutting edge and crystallize solutions instantly because you are centered on best serving your team.

"**Synergy** reflects building a team so that the results of the group exceed the individual efforts. To create synergy all the time is another big part of leading people. It is pulling everybody together, or you're going to have so many fractured pieces."

Mike Vrabel, outside linebacker for the New England Patriots inspires confidence in others by his example. He takes action!

Mike further explains his perception of leadership:

Vrabel:
> "A leader is the one held accountable in the end. So being accountable and consistent day in and day out earns respect. You don't have to be the most productive player or person, but it certainly helps.
>
> "Those same leadership skills belong to team members, whether in sports, business, or family, who understand the tremendous explosion of potential in the synergy of caring members. Individual accolades follow the winning attitude and team success."

CONCLUSION

From the leaders' comments in my lineup, each one was influenced in their younger years. Each leader was willing to learn and put in their time to perfect their skills and performance. However, achieving skills is only one third of the leadership formula. As Vermeil so aptly stated, leadership is about building relationships, the second part of the leadership formula. In this book, part of our leadership attitude is serving, helping and being available to empower others to their greatness. How to do this is part three of the leadership formula: leading through consistent action, positive attitude, and infectious confidence.

CHAPTER TWO

Leadership is a Choice, Not a Position

The fundamentals of Success and Leadership
are not rocket science.
They are, however, missed by most people.

Rudy Giuliani

Football figures in the limelight become the examples of leadership for the up-and-coming generations of sports enthusiasts and dreamers. Whether these figures excel in physical prowess, mental skills, management, or coaching abilities, they are innovators—leaders by choice who demonstrate admirable attitude and action. What are the responsibilities of such leaders to their audiences?

- Realize that others want to be like you, but may not make the effort as you did. They want to be where you are, but wouldn't want to do what it took to get there.

- Inspire others to get the most out of what they have.

- Keep in mind the well-being of those who follow you.

- Realize their learning requires repetition.

- Maintain your standards, and be aware of the standards that others have set for you.

ATTITUDES AND BEHAVIORS

One level of a leader's responsibility, then, is to know what you bring to the leadership position in terms of attitudes. The second level of responsibility is to model behaviors that spur others to excellence. Quarterback Danny Wuerffel demonstrates both such attitude and actions.

Danny won the Heisman Trophy as quarterback for the University of Florida in 1996 and was drafted by the New Orleans Saints in 1997. Wuerffel also played for the Green Bay Packers, Chicago Bears, and the Washington Redskins before retiring from his NFL career. Danny currently serves as the executive director of Desire Street Ministries, which "exists to train and send leaders to revitalize impoverished neighborhoods through spiritual and community development." As a living example of leadership, Danny indicates, "Through a leader's unique style, he or she can help other people be better than they would be by themselves."

Those living examples of leadership are conscientious people who are aware of their style, how they interact with people, and how they affect others. In the next chapter, you can determine what your leadership style is.

AWARENESS

Morten Andersen always says, "You need to be aware. If you're a confident person, you carry yourself a certain way and you talk a certain way. You act a certain way."

In my first book, *Life's a Snap!* I talked of how leaders carry themselves with awareness and a positive viewpoint. A leader's confidence is the assurance that you can succeed, and it is infectious. An aware player in the game of life can read his own emotions and sense his moods. He can shift to the mood needed in any situation, like being upbeat in a team meeting, inspirational in a speech, or aggressive on the field.

Another example of awareness is trusting yourself to know how to respond when things aren't going as well as you'd like. You literally have to be fearless and, ultimately, trust your training and instinct to take over.

INSPIRE

Most people fear the unknown. The leader's challenge is to inspire courage to face the unknown. Fear is a positive emotion that can empower movement quickly toward success, overcoming the challenges that you face. When you feel fear or pressure, you have two choices, which are to act hastily or to act with awareness.

- Acting hastily scatters your action and diffuses your effectiveness.

- Acting with awareness moves you forward with more respect. You watch and you discern. On the field, where the game moves fast, every individual player knows their task well with practiced efficiency. Their teammates know what to expect, and the coach watches for expected outcomes.

Trent Green was inspired to leadership by the challenge from his basketball coach.

Green:

"I was ten years old, in fifth grade, and I realized that I wasn't in a small town in the Illinois cornfields any more. My family moved to the big city of St. Louis, and I was on several select basketball teams. I knew nothing of being a leader. I just was doing what I do—being kind of single-focused on my skills. The youth basketball coach pulled me to the side of the court and said, 'Hey, whether or not you know it, you're the leader on this team. Guys follow you based on how you practice, how you approach the game, how you approach practices.'

"Now, I'd been there only three weeks, and these kids had played together for several years. The coach caught me off guard. For someone that's only ten years old, I wasn't really ready for that. I had always been focused on doing my part and getting it done."

Indeed, the coach inspired Trent to rise to the challenge. There were times in practice when Trent didn't feel like doing drills, but because everybody else was looking to him, he had to follow through and say to himself, "I've got to get through this." The challenging self-talk worked and fueled his positive attitude and action.

CONFIDENCE

Football is the number one sport in the United States. Pressures are high and intense. Players play for the love of money, love of family, or love of the game. It's a pressure cooker and a "what have you done for me lately?" profession in which one performs or perishes.

The pressure never lets up. If you aren't performing at the necessary level, you run a high chance of being cut, released from the team. If you do perform at the necessary level, you have to keep pace every week. Pressure builds throughout the season.

It's December, you're in the playoff hunt. The spotlight is brighter, the focus more defined. The team makes the playoffs. The regular season is now only a distant memory. The playoffs come. Every game is now a national game. Win and go on, lose and go home.

Do you ever look at some players and think that nothing affects them? No matter how intense the situation, they seem to respond as though nothing gets to them. Tom Brady is a good example as a three time Super Bowl Champion and recipient of two Super Bowl MVP awards. At times he may look robotic; at other moments, he's butting heads with his offensive lineman before a game winning drive.

But a few things remain constant—he's prepared and he is confident in his abilities. Tom got his chance after Drew Bledsoe went down with an injury in the middle of the season. All Tom did was perform, and at a high level. He was prepared; he made the most of his opportunities. It would have been easy for him to think he was a career backup. After all, he was a sixth-round pick, not exactly the place from which franchise quarterbacks are taken. But he prepared like a starter, and when his time came, he performed like one as well.

As teammate Mike Vrabel said about their first Super Bowl win, and the game winning drive that

Tom led, "Our QB threw five or six check downs in the final drive...and we went down and scored." He took what was given, and didn't try to make plays that weren't there. It wasn't about him personally; it was about the success of the team. Critics might say he was making the safe pass. Those safe passes won them a championship.

It was where his skills were at that time, and he was doing what his body and mind instinctively told him to do because of the preparation beforehand. Trent Green comments:

Green:

"You've got to remember, Tom was really young that first year when they won it all. You know that you're hitting your check downs because maybe you're not as comfortable with the progression. So instead of going four progressions and hitting your check down, maybe you're going two and hitting your check down. So some of that is just the comfort zone of the pocket. I don't want to speak for Tom, but you get to a point where it's not as risky to throw that ball in between three defenders as it was when you were just some guy on the street, because it's like if you were throwing a pick then and cost the game. The ramifications are substantially different then if you do it now."

Now, in subsequent years, Brady evolved, like all team members strive to do. Green explains further:

23

Green:

> "He's throwing down the field more. I think he passed that check out stage.... trying not to make any mistakes. He's trying to make a play and put the pressure on the defense. We evolved from a team that has to play a certain way to win to now...trying to be more aggressive."

Most of the time it's very difficult and very involved to make something look "easy." The key is confidence.

CONFIDENCE

Confidence in yourself, your teammates, and your leadership is a necessity. The belief deep down that you are up to the task cannot be conjured. A player may be able to fool people for a while, but eventually he is exposed if he can't truly handle it. The one person that ultimately can't be fooled is you.

Develop inner belief in yourself through your confidence. As Morten Andersen says, "You can be confident without being arrogant. To me, arrogant is degrading to yourself, your skill, and your cause. I think confidence is a beautiful thing to have, especially in a leadership role."

During one Chiefs' game preparation for playing Philadelphia, I felt a few coaches on the staff seemed scared, or at least a little intimidated by the skills available and presented by many of the Eagles' players. They were emphasizing how good Philadelphia was, and the message to us as players seemed defensive about our preparation. Vermeil was running the risk of showing a lack of confidence.

The next day, Vermeil must have caught wind of the players' frustration because he did an about-face in attitude and message from the previous day of giving too much credit to Philadelphia. "They have to come in here and play us. They're the ones who should be scared."

The message didn't take with the Chiefs. During the game, we were up 17 to 0 and then ended up losing a game that we shouldn't have lost. Philly was good, but in my opinion, our mindset from the get-go was that we would have a tough time winning. In my analysis, once the Chiefs were ahead, we didn't play to win. We played to not lose, and there is a huge difference between the two! How do you play in the game of life? Do you play to get by? I hope you play to win!

When you defend your position, attitude, or strategies, you run the risk of showing a lack of confidence in your actions and game plan. On the other hand, your confidence carries you through the pressures you face. Give your opponent respect, but nothing more. Don't build them up too much in your mind, and more importantly, in the minds of those you are leading.

Just like most businesses, no matter how proficient you are, someone is probably raising the bar,

25

pushing you to get better, and confidence is the one leadership trait that carries you through these pressures.

ESTABLISHING TRUST

Leadership is a position of trust because others expect a leader to be honorable and responsible. Those who rely on a leader expect consistent and dependable behaviors. For example, Del Rio explains that, "Coaches and players have to trust each other, and it isn't blind trust. We constantly work on respectful attitudes in this climate. Much comes down to the trust factor.

Del Rio has shared his take on the "trust factor":

Del Rio:

"At the coaching level, we work hard to establish that the players understand or know how we do things that we need to do. I think when players see that we're all about helping them be at their best on Sunday game days, they know we're helping them maximize their abilities. When the players believe in themselves and their coach, they feel that trust, and they give you their all. One of the goals of a coach or of a good leader is to push and prod the players beyond where they're capable of going on their own."

Wuerffel adds this story of trust.

Wuerffel:

"At the last meeting before the last preseason game of a team that I was with, a coach gave one of the most impassioned speeches that I'd heard. His first point was that football was about trusting the guy next to you, like being in a foxhole. You're only as good as the guys in this room, and nobody else cares and this whole brotherhood requires loyalty that we have to protect at all costs. Showing trust and loyalty to team members is the only way to win."

POSITIVE ENERGY

The ability to sustain a positive attitude is paramount as a leader; moreover, the ability to sustain a positive energy with your team, family, or coworkers requires a special awareness. Del Rio explains:

Del Rio:

"I know that I believe in positive energy. I believe in coming to work everyday with a smile on my face, enjoying what I do, feeling blessed with the opportunity.

"I believe that it's imperative that a leader have conviction, and that he follow those convictions. There's no question that you're going to be faced with adversity, whether it's business or in sports. People will question you, so you have to have strong beliefs in faith and what you're doing." Faith, facing adversity, conviction—these are life circumstances that require positive energy and focus.

Positive energy comes through in different attitudes and actions. Here are five positive energy keys that I use every day to stay upbeat.

1. Being cheerful.
2. Being grateful.
3. Greeting each person with a smile.
4. Showing appreciation.
5. Breathing to stay calm.

None of us exists in a vacuum. We are members of a team, whether in the NFL, with our families, or in corporations or small businesses. Our attitudes, moods, and words affect each other. We can help each other feel upbeat and supported or drained and tired. We want to play with others who radiate the charisma and confidence of positive energy because it motivates and inspires.

☑ DEL RIO ON POSITIVE ENERGY IN LEADERSHIP

"I love our guys, and I love what I'm doing. They feel that positive energy in understanding that I can help them be better on Sundays. That's one of the core beliefs that I have: Surround yourself with good people who love to play, love to compete. If we can convince them that we have an ability to help them be better on Sundays, then they're going to soak up every bit of coaching that we have. Mutual respect and positive energy are coaching traits that motivate."

28

PROVIDE CRUCIAL FEEDBACK

A leader is responsible for providing feedback to his team members. At the same time, this leader would welcome, and even expect, people who put their opinions on the table, even if those opinions happens to differ from their own.

Del Rio:

"One of the things I saw in New Orleans with Mike Ditka was that we had several staff members, who would say, 'Yeah, coach, you're right.' They were the 'yes' men.

"I do everything I can to empower my staff to speak their mind, and I want to know ahead of time. Don't bring in the information that you have once the draft is over. Don't bring it in on Monday after the ball game. When you're asked an opinion, feel empowered to give that opinion."

If a coach or team leader doesn't know what is in your head or heart, they have no chance to respond with good information. Our coaching responsibility is to empower a player to maximize his abilities, to put team members in position to do what they know best. This requires crucial feedback.

When a leader provides a plan and team members know their expectations and goals, this serves as a structure for providing effective feedback.

A leader cannot provide feedback without specificity. For example, when a little leaguer says, "I can't catch," my job is to find out the specific skill that makes him not catch. When a teenager at one of my talks says, "I want to be better at snapping," I can provide feedback when the teen identifies the specific long-snapping skill, like holding the ball or focusing his aim, that he wants to improve.

The feedback process is a dialogue that requires time for listening and discussion.

☑ DEL RIO ON SUPPORTING STRENGTHS

"A lot of times, there's a negative vibe that I've experienced as a player. As a coach, I've also witnessed coaches complain about what their players can't do. I think it's our job as leaders to understand what team members may have trouble with, minimize the exposure they're going to have in those situations, and maximize the exposure and success they're going to have in situations where they can shine.

The key is knowing their strengths. It seems like in the world today, all we look for is the negatives. Why can't we see the positive rather than the negative and try to accentuate those more?"

Perhaps the more humorous incident of providing crucial feedback was when Coach Cowher observed one of my snaps. In my first book, *Life's A SNAP*, I thanked Coach Cowher for thickening my skin because I was fortunate to have him as a coach. There were certainly times when his feedback made me angry because I think at times Coach Cowher would check the rookies' and veterans' psyches to see how we responded to things. Here is one example of providing crucial feedback without words.

I had a low snap in a game several years into my career with the Steelers. The snap was a bit low, but nothing bad happened because of it, luckily. However, it was not a good snap, and no one was more irritated by me than me. Usually Coach Cowher would come over, get on me a little and tell me to go back and practice. After this particular low snap, out of the corner of my eye, I could see him coming. The moment he approached me, I turned, looked him in the eye, and said, "I know, the bleepin' snap was low."

Cowher just kind of looked at me, smiled, and laughed before he walked off. He never said a word about it. Boy, that was crucial feedback to me. We silently agreed that we both understood, and I don't think he ever said anything to me again through games. Maybe he thought "this guy is growing up a little." Or maybe he knew I took accountability for my actions. Either way, I would like to believe there was a healthy respect for what I was doing for the team as the long snapper.

As a leader, you eventually want people who are working so well together that you don't always have to provide critical feedback. In a trusting and respectful relationship, a leader wants team members who are inspired and motivated by their internal forces to succeed at their game. I mean, if they're truly bothered by their actions, if they're not up to par, then you really don't have to do anything, because they are going to do it themselves.

STAY THE COURSE

In the NFL, we all realize that winning is the ultimate goal. Only one team ultimately achieves the desired success, and no team goes through a season without dealing with a loss. Yet, we all must persist. The concept of winning holds true in the business world because no business owner wants to lose assets. In the family, the principle that holds family members together, functioning as a team when facing adversity, is staying the course or being persistent.

In 2007, Will Shields announced his retirement after fourteen seasons with the Kansas City Chiefs and after starting in 230 straight games as an offensive guard. It was a team record and the second longest consecutive starting streak in the NFL behind QB Brett Favre of the Green Bay Packers. Hailing from the University of Nebraska, Shields was the third-round pick in the 1993 NFL draft, and went to the Pro Bowl every year since 1995. He went to his twelfth Pro Bowl in 2007, a Chiefs' team record.

Playing for the NFL is incredibly hard on the human body. Players who last past the first few years have injuries and chronic pain that plague them for the rest of their lives. With more than fourteen years on the field, Will stayed his course despite starting many games in great pain, which he simply had to endure. Few people outside of the training staff knew. He was a leader who never really tried to set a record. Yet his leadership traits carried him forward to win with his team. He was so talented, such a leader, that that's just what he did.

Even more amazing are his activities off the field. Will won the Walter Payton Man of the Year, the highest honor the NFL gives for off-field achievement for the foundation he created, The Will to Succeed Foundation. One project that was dear to the foundation member's hearts was "Operation Breakthrough," which serves low-income children from single families and the homeless. It is run by the St. Vincent's Family Service Center in Kansas City.

How a leader deals with failure through persistence defines his ability to face adversity and continue to be successful.

- Persistence is moving along steadily despite obstacles.

- Persistence is continuing goal-directed action despite difficulties or discouragement.

- Persistence is the ability to maintain action regardless of your feelings. You press on even when you feel like quitting.

- Persistence is a state of mind, through which you hold your focus on what you are doing, despite adversity and inconvenience, especially when it may not be easy.

- Persistence is staying the course despite the odds.

ACTIONS

One of my favorite book titles is *Just Do It!* (April 1995) because it states so well the essence of becoming successful in life or as a professional football player. NFL players, like other focused athletes, epitomize the practice of taking action, day in and day out, to succeed in their game plan. Focused, daily action leads to consistent success for students completing homework or entrepreneurs marketing their business. Consistent action steps taken by a leader, especially in the NFL, provide a visible example to the rest of us.

This leads to self-leadership that becomes a practice, a daily habit of taking the right action. Leadership is also a decision to act. Within the realm of a leader's actions are character traits for leadership.

RESPONSIBILITY

The person I know who most exemplifies these leadership traits is Trent Green. In 2003, the Kansas

City Chiefs were 9-0. The streak was growing and so was the media attention on his ability to lead the Chiefs. *Sports Illustrated* featured Green on the November 17th, 2003 cover.

Trent leads in a way unique to NFL players. I've observed his ability to guide the entire team. In a conversation with KCC defensive lineman, Eric Hicks, on the way home from a Cincinnati game (yes, we carpool), he commented on how Trent always took the time to be personable, to talk and joke with everyone, from the superstars down to the practice squad players.

We can learn from Trent's leadership style. As a quarterback, he will never be on special teams or take offensive or defensive perspectives. He sees the members and the whole team; one helps the other, and each affects the other. Special teams affects field position. Field position affects play-calling decisions. Defense affects not only play calling, but also how soon the offense gets back on the field.

Trent's personal style involves associating with everybody and anybody. He is very even handed in his leadership approach. He respects others, as he desires to be respected. There are no "favorites" with Trent.

Like Trent, leaders in any profession would do well to understand the benefits of personal relationships with those they mentor. Through such friendships grows credibility.

CREDIBILITY

The person growing into a leadership position has to earn their due. This seems to be the structure or nature of organizational culture. Earning one's due has two components. The first is *what* a person achieves, the second is *how* they achieve it.

Establishing credibility means that you know what to do, when it needs to be done, and you do it, consistently. Credibility and consistency walk hand in hand because if you are consistent, people will know they can rely upon you and will trust you. In the eyes of your team members, trust equals credibility. Even with this, you don't always get things right, but you develop the process of what it takes to be successful and how it needs to be done, all the time.

Once a leader has achievements behind them, their identity becomes associated with the acts, not the person. Accomplishments don't define people, and a top player can get lost in their fans' applause and appreciation. Football is what I do, not who I am.

I play the roles of father, NFL snapper, husband, and trusted friend. Within these roles, certain qualities remain consistent and have established my credibility with my children, team, wife, and friends.

I do what I say I will do.

I do it when it needs to be done.

I practice this behavior consistently.

Make a plan for what you wish to accomplish, but don't forget who you are while doing it.

PREPARATION

Are you a true pro? Do you work hard so you never get it wrong? The NFL is a high-pressure, high-performance business. Just like other professions, this one comes with high expectations. As players, we are brought to the NFL because of beliefs that we can perform at this national level.

High pressure, high expectations, and high performance, however, are not the domain of only NFL players. What new mother hasn't felt the pressure and expectation to provide tender nurturing to her child? What dad hasn't faced his worst fears for his children's safety? What corporate worker hasn't felt squeezed under deadlines? Each of us as parent, entrepreneur, and coach or team member needs the skill of preparation and practice because it is the way we learn. Our skills empower us to become the expert at what we do in life, and we constantly practice our skills.

- Before I deliver a speech, I rehearse my performance.

- Before my son went to a new school, we visited first so he had an image in his mind. He could place himself there.

- Before a business meeting, I prepare my agenda.

- Before game day, you can bet every coach quizzes his team on the plays.

In leadership roles today, approaching tasks by trial and error doesn't cut it. Each of us was brought onto some team in order to get the job done. In the NFL, these questions are answered first during training camp and then throughout the season. *Can you do it consistently at a high level? Are you the "true pro?" Do you work hard with the thought of never doing it wrong?*

Preparation brings freedom. How? When you realize that you're up to what's being asked of you, the ultimate result is an exuberance and total ability to deal with stress or pressure effectively. There are, of course, other strategies that players use to deal with stress, but if one isn't supremely confident in their own skills or abilities, nothing else makes up for it.

TAKING RISKS

Gridiron leadership requires taking risks. Some leaders encourage risk-taking, yet not all people are risk-takers because they deem the behavior too risky. What is the difference between taking risks and engaging in risky behavior?

Being too risky means you haven't calculated the consequence of your behavior. You may not be aware of your limits, the circumstances, or your resources. For example, some adults do not have financial management skills and spend money they do not have through credit cards. They establish large indebtedness by not understanding risks. People who engage in risky behavior have little vision or understanding of the long-term consequences, or the domino effect, so to speak.

On the other hand, a risk taker makes a move or a decision based upon calculated results. The results will have a good probability of success. How does taking risks look in NFL leaders?

A coach finds a rookie with new talent and is willing to risk time, emotional involvement, and working closely to hone future leaders. We define a great coach as one who demonstrates commitment to his team. We define a willing player as one who takes risks effectively to advance the team.

RESILIENCE

Morten Andersen's star rose at Michigan State. Today, as a leader and an NFL veteran of twenty-five years, Andersen believes that leaders are born with certain strong temperaments. On the other hand, leaders also learn much of leadership abilities while they mentor others throughout their lives.

Andersen:
"When one enters the NFL, he will never be the same. You stretch beyond your comfort zone and improve, or

you try harder, or you drop out." Some people simply don't stretch beyond their comfort zone, and that is when you see their energy and interest in life slowly wane. No matter how life treats you, a leader seems to have the resilience to weather the storm.

"Know these coping mechanisms that you learn through such experiences are valuable and makes you an even stronger person and leader because you've felt deeper changes in your body, soul, spirit. You've persevered through adversity's lessons, distasteful though they may have been. I think it's healthy as a human being, and especially for a leader.

"If you're going to talk the talk, then walk the walk. A leader has to be able to do that almost 100 percent of the time. A leader has to master that.

"I try to master my craft. I spend a lot of time on my personal skill and technique development, on my personal excellence. Leadership is what I learned from Frank Ganz Sr in Atlanta. He had a great saying that I enjoy and still carry with me in my pocket: 'Powerful, productive relationship is based on powerful productive communication.'"

Like in family or in business, if you want to improve, then you seek new methods. You must be fearless in making mistakes. No mistakes mean no learning is happening.

Frank Ganz, Sr. was named NFL special teams coach of the year twice. Frank is known for his unique ability to relate to and inspire players. Anyone who has ever played for him will mention his uncanny ability to relate stories to the task at hand. While Frank himself never coached me, I spent five years with his son, Frank Jr.

Frank Sr. was a regular at training camps in Wisconsin during my days with the Chiefs. Coach Vermeil brought him in to address our team. Coach Dick Vermeil refers to Frank as the finest coach he's ever been around. His love of the game shows, even to this day, as he returned to coaching on February 20, 2008, at the age of seventy. He will be coaching special teams for the SMU Mustangs under head coach June Jones.

Resilience is the ability to bounce back after facing pressure, trauma, or resistance. For a child who falls off a horse during a riding lesson, resilience is getting back on the horse immediately and trying again. In an NFL game, resilience is speedy recovery time and rushing to the next play with full focus and mental clarity. For a corporate leader, resilience is more involved.

According to the Global Resiliency Network, "[Corporate] resilience is a twofold capacity. It includes both the skillful anticipation and preparation for change as well as the ability to respond effectively to the unexpected as it happens."[i]

As Coach Vermeil says, "The good leaders I've been around, whom I've learned from, were able to take adversity and utilize it to get better, rather than to pull themselves down. Invariably whenever any team is successful, your success will be directly related to how well you handle the adversity in building that team." This is also true in businesses and families. Team members carry each other through those hard times.

CONSISTENCY

As a leader, you need to present a clear, concise message. Be consistent. All people thrive on consistency. Inconsistency in leadership behaviors by a parent, coach, or executive causes confusion, frustration, and anger. Imagine how a child feels when one day Mom said she could stay home from school, and the next day Mom said she had to go to school. The child would awaken each morning wondering what the plan would be.

Imagine what Coach Herm Edwards would do if my snaps were inconsistent from game to game. In his leadership capacity, Coach Edwards is consistent, and his team appreciates that leadership trait. He's been charged with the task of leading the Kansas City Chiefs—leading leaders, leading egos.

Consistency has applications at different levels. For example, think about the behavior of someone whom you'd consider bad, and also a person you think of as good. Your perception of their behavior is based on long-term observation. You have seen consistency in a behavioral pattern.

- Thus at the personal level, leaders are consistently good in what they do, how they act, and what they communicate.

- Leaders are consistent in behavior over time. Anyone can shine in their moment of glory, but are they consistent over longer periods? Leaders are consistent in all areas of their lives.

COMMUNICATION

Of all the character traits of leaders, communication is the foundation for effectiveness. People judge each other by their ability to convey ideas, the clarity of conviction, and the inspiring rhetoric. In other words, without communication, there is no leadership. Followers watch leaders for their:

- Communication style
- Attitude toward their audience
- Level of knowledge about the subject
- Emotional tone

A leader's communication strategy is about making effective changes or causing a desired result. In between the phases of speaking and listening, is an opportunity for learning. A parent wants to see successful and respectful behaviors. An executive wants to motivate accountability and contribution.

A coach wants to drive points and win.

Ray Lewis was a number one pick of the Baltimore Ravens in 1996. Ray's incredible skills have earned the former Miami Hurricane linebacker nine selections to the Pro Bowl as well as playing and winning the Super Bowl XXXV Championship. The Associated Press also named Lewis NFL Defensive Player of The Year in 2000 and 2003.

While Lewis is known for his tenacious plays on the field, he is also know for the leadership he provides. He is the heart and soul of the Baltimore Ravens franchise. His antics as he is introduced before home games in Baltimore are legendary, and often time consuming. Whether you agree with his theatrics or not, you cannot deny the fact that he inspires and fires up not only his team, but the tens of thousands of Ravens fans there to support their team. His passion for the game shines and his goal of being the best is evident in his demeanor on the field.

For example, Del Rio explains his approach to one player's attitude and actions.

Del Rio:

"When I was in Baltimore with Ray Lewis, he was a great player when we first arrived, but he made selfish choices during the ball game. Where he was such a good playmaker, he would want to make every play. As a result, he would be out of position and give up some big plays.

"I've talked a lot with him, particularly in the first

year, about the importance of him being there for his teammates, of not losing that ability to be a playmaker and be productive, but to understand that you have a responsibility to the team.

"I said, 'Other guys are watching you, and as the leader of the team, if you're not doing the right things and you're not accountable, it's very difficult to lead others.' I challenged him to understand the impact that a great player can have. Great players affect other players and help them achieve at a higher level. So I think in that time he grew in that area. Obviously, he was a great player before I got there, and is a great player now, but I think I had an impact on his ability to be a leader."

COMMUNICATION GUIDELINES

☑ Don't be too intimidated to speak your mind.

☑ Speak up about what you agree with and what you disagree with.

☑ Foster mutual respect and trust.

☑ State expectations clearly.

☑ Back the goals or expectations with feedback forms, grade sheets.

☑ Emphasize problems that could be mental errors or lack of technique.

In my years with Coach Vermeil and the Kansas City Chiefs, I remember the clarity and honesty of Vermeil's communication with me when he came on board. "I don't know if I want you here, Kendall. I want somebody who can do more than what you do, and as is the case with all coaches, I want a long snapper who could play another position."

Coach Vermeil was the first person to actually say that to me. Now I knew everybody thought that; but as a leader, you get a lot more credibility when you tell the truth, even if it's not what the person wants to hear.

A leader demonstrates their credibility with honesty. As Vermeil says, "Once you become trustworthy, then regardless of whether the conversation is either positive or negative, it will be a worthwhile conversation to both sides."

CONCLUSION

Leadership is a choice, and in my experience, a young person chooses leadership when they honor someone's confidence in them, step up, and play the game to the best of their ability. Then training for their position and place in life starts because they risked a part of themselves to embrace a vision bigger than themselves. Of all the leadership traits in this chapter, I find awareness to be the foundation skill that allows a leader to know him or herself as well as understand others. In the next chapter, discovering your leadership style is an essential step in self-awareness.

CHAPTER THREE

Leadership Styles

Mental toughness is many things and rather difficult
to explain. It qualities are sacrifice and self-denial.
Also, more importantly, it is combined with a perfectly
disciplined will that refuses to give in. It's a state of
mind. You could call it character in action.

Vince Lombardi

Business and leadership books, including
the *U.S. Army Handbook* (1973), divide leadership
styles into the three traditional modes: autocratic,
democratic, or laissez-faire. The autocratic leader
is the head honcho who directs and expects. The
democratic leader involves his team in the decision-
making process, and the laissez-faire leader delegates
decision-making because he trusts his team to know
their jobs better than he does. Each style in decades

past has had its place, based upon the relationships of the leader to his community. Also, in the traditional sense, leaders have been expected to be so flexible they can shift roles based upon the context and situation.

We've come a long way from these traditional models of leadership and the concept that one leader must be all things to all people. Research studies in human development and personality models suggest that all of us enter this world with a specific temperament pattern, which is genetics' contribution to who we are.

However, who we become is a combination of our interaction and adaptation to our environment, which consists of people, tasks, stressors, emotional anchors, social teachers, and other cultural influences. In this chapter we are discussing nature's component, personal style, meaning, "I'm born this way." In addition, we understand that training, education, and experiences contribute to who we become and how we respond to life.

The leading expert in this field who commands my respect is Ken Keis, president and CEO of Consulting Resource Group International, Inc. (CRG). More than 1 million people in twenty countries and eight languages have engaged CRG assessments and resources to enrich their lives, leadership, and communities. Keis is also a certified personal coach and stays in the forefront of the field of leadership. His views contribute to this chapter.

PERSONAL STYLES

Leadership styles stem from your personal style. Keis explains, "Personal style is your natural predisposition to perceive, approach, and interact with your environment, which includes time, people, tasks, and situations." After conducting more than 2,000 training programs and writing about leadership for more than twenty years, Keis is convinced "that without a full understanding of your personal style—and the personal style of everyone with whom you interact—you are missing critical knowledge that can contribute to fulfillment for all team members. It's like flying a plane in a dense fogbank. Without training in aircraft instrumentation, you are living by a hope and a prayer that you can make it to a safe landing site. That is the way most people live their lives. It is the difference between leading by accident or with intention."

Keis is not speaking of just your perception of how you lead. He is talking about an innate temperament that guides the course of our interactions with people and the environment. In the first chapter, we've discussed the qualities of coaches and other players who have influenced our growth and performance. In Chapter Two are listed the attitudes and actions that top coaches and players feel are necessary to make it in the game, on and off the field. One of those key attitudes was the ability to build credibility with others. Our credibility increases or decreases based on how we interact with others. Personal style is key to understanding yourself as well as building credibility with your team members, partner, children, and business colleagues.

Coaches understand what makes players tick. Parents often intuit their children's responses and needs to help them negotiate school and peer group pressures. Here is Keis' explanation:

Keis:

"It's a biological fact that we are born with a natural predisposition to a distinct personal style. It's not something we can choose to avoid. We take our personal style with us, everywhere we go. Research confirms that each of us has unique and specific style preferences at birth. From that moment, our personal style starts to play a powerful role in our lives by influencing our activities."

- Choosing supportive child-care environments
- Parenting style
- Learning and instructional styles that meet your specific needs
- Selecting the right job and understanding job-style fit
- Accepting the differences in yourself and others
- Getting along better with your life partner
- Coaching others

- Customer service, sales, and leadership
- Having the confidence to reject feelings of guilt and the pressures to change from those who are different than you are. That includes peer pressure, parents, and teachers.
- Building teams that complement your business needs
- Starting a business
- Hiring and promoting
- Resolving conflict

Everybody has all four of the leadership styles we will discuss, but at different levels or intensities. The higher the score or intensity in one style, the more you are wired and likely to respond to your world. A leader tends to lead with his preferred style, or the most intense style. Yet a follower responds to a leader who appeals to the follower's preferences. A child will respond to a parent whom he feels understands and connects with him. A client will respond to a business or personal coach who builds an immediate rapport.

As the coaches in this book have reiterated, the coach or leader must know what they bring to the game, and they must know the style of their players to motivate their skill-building and inspire them to win. A follower, a player, a child, or a worker will always remind us, "I will follow you when you meet my needs, not your needs, first." Thus, an aware and conscious leader always asks some key questions:

- What is my personal style since my leadership style stems from it?
- How do I interact with people whose styles are different from mine?
- How do I get tasks done? What is my approach?
- Can I actually be conscious and aware at any given moment of my leadership style and the styles of the individuals I'm trying to lead?
- How can I appeal to them in the best way to be able to motivate and inspire them? That means that I need to meet their needs as much as mine.

WHAT IS YOUR LEADERSHIP STYLE?

As previously mentioned, we each have all four personal styles, but at varying levels of intensity. This is called blended style. Eighty-five percent of us have blended styles. Only 10 to 15 percent of the population stands out with one strong personal style of leadership. Here are the four basic styles.

BEHAVIORAL LEADERS

Behavioral leaders are action and results oriented. They rise into leadership easily with the following characteristics.

- A desire to achieve
- Extremely strategic
- Solution oriented
- Work rapidly
- Forget what's happened in the past
- Focus on present results and how to move forward
- Dislike those who waste their time

When leaders are under stress, they might think they are on a losing streak or the game plan isn't going well. Their response to stress is to double their efforts. They show a lot of endurance as far as their capacity to handle a lot of stimulus, information, and tasks that are going on simultaneously. Behavioral leaders will assume authority. This can be a tricky character trait to manage as they risk coming across as arrogant, rather than confident. Sometimes they can be so intense that they overwhelm others. This forcefulness and impatience can reduce team members' willingness to participate because they don't want to be chewed out or belittled. Another trait is that behavioral leaders can be seen as insensitive to other people's feelings, because they're driving toward the goal, moving forward, and it really doesn't matter what you think or feel.

Oddly enough, because this leader is driven, caught up in activities, and works harder when under stress, he can be lonely, holding up the flag alone. This intensity and drive can be at the expense of their relationships both professionally and personally.

COGNITIVE LEADERS

Cognitive leaders are of the second personal style called cognitive analysis and demonstrate the following traits.

- Quality oriented
- Analytical
- Focus on the past as well as the future— thinking behind and forward, and not present.
- Can be perfectionists and finicky about a specific point

Assistant coaches or other team members can fall into these analytical roles because they understand the different plays, the mistakes, and can coach the necessary skills. They also have the gift of seeing what's not there, as in knowing where a play or team process breaks down. The flipside of that skill is that a cognitive leader could nitpick on one aspect, skill, or performance, and this is demoralizing for the rookie or player.

Cognitive leaders can learn to emphasize what is right and show appreciation for the team or family member's efforts. Emphasize the skill and explain what's not there. What can be done to improve the opportunity? Include the opportunities for improvement as well as approval in conversations and relationships.

Cognitive leaders are cautious and careful. As rationalists, they carefully think through options and choices as ensuring quality is one of their gifts. They follow standards and directives. So even if I'm coaching somebody in this area, they'll be able to follow the focus. They do have the ability for critical analysis and the ability to debrief. Sometimes, however, they get too bogged down in details and can lose time by overanalyzing things, getting stuck in the paralysis of analysis. Their self worth is derived from the quality of the work they do. Finally, they have the gift to see what is missing or what is not right. But they need to balance feedback to others, because if the focus is always on what was not done right, the result could be demoralizing, and ultimately affect performance.

They can take criticism personally and this weakness could reduce their ability to engage. While cognitive leaders can be perfectionists, they can also learn to not sweat the insignificant stuff.

INTERPERSONAL-HARMONY STYLE LEADERS

Interpersonal-harmony style includes leaders and followers who have the great ability to emotionally connect with other people, wherever they're at. Their personal qualities make them excellent with different personal styles as far as reliability, compassion, and great listening skills.

- They have this intuitive sensing radar of where you are emotionally. They know and feel you. Of all leadership styles, they have the greatest ability to be here now, to be attentive to the task at hand.
- They promote balance and harmony.
- They're very practical.
- They try to adapt to stress, meaning they defer to the group and they will put other people's needs ahead of theirs.

Now the flipside of those skills is they put other people's needs ahead of their own at their consequence or cost, meaning they over-commit. In some parenting situations, mom or dad could make themselves a victim of their own compassion when they defer to others too often, and compassion becomes a fault. Thus, such a person could be taken for granted and under-appreciated. Because they value harmony, they are not confrontational and avoid conflict.

Interpersonal-harmony leaders can learn to stand up for themselves. While they dislike arguments, difficult decisions, firings, or accountability areas, they need to stretch and develop the skills to be confrontational when required. The reason they want to avoid conflict is because this can disturb them physically, actually causing distress in their body and possibly even taking them out emotionally. This is one of the areas that they need to manage to ensure that they can hold others accountable while not creating any long-term negative physical or mental impact to themselves.

AFFECTIVE STYLE LEADERS

Affective style, in its purest stance or leadership style is affective-expressive. These are individuals who love people and seek to influence. You'll see this leadership style in sports commentators because they are very fluid verbally. Affective-expressive leaders have:

- An intuitive sense
- A creative side
- High energy
- Eternal optimism
- Great networking skills

When these leaders encounter stress, they need an

escape route for a while, so they might go to the movies or kind of hang out. They are in the present and into the future. They sense other people's feelings, and in a lot of cases, they get their energy from being around those people. In other words, these are not individuals who like to work alone. They like to be a part of groups and be connected to them. They can inspire and influence others toward their capabilities, because they weave stories of encouragement around what's going on. So an affective leader's gift is inspiring other people to tune up toward their potential.

On the other hand, difficulties these leaders may encounter in their style include time immersion. They can lose track of time. They're so into what they're doing, they don't have this consciousness of time. The other tendency is that they burn out because they go at tasks with gusto. Another challenge for this leadership style is to learn when to be quiet. They can sell something and then buy it back. In other words, there are times when saying less does a lot more. Saying nothing can often accomplish what long-winded speeches cannot.

People with affective-expressive styles can be egotistical and self-absorbed. In their perception, it's about them; it's not about you. So they do have a tendency to be more self-centered and self-absorbed than the other styles. They tend to not like rules or structure. These mavericks have a lot of creativity and energy to bring to a team as long as they develop personal discipline in their interactions with self and others.

WHO'S IN CONTROL?

In Chapter Two, I emphasized the value of leaders being aware, and this skill enables leaders to know when they are in control of their leadership style or when their style is in control of them.

- A leader is in control of his style when he cultivates his strengths and does not indulge his weaknesses. Rather, he understands areas that he does not prefer to operate in as opportunities for learning and personal growth.

- A leader is not in control when he uses his style as an excuse for his behavior and when the challenges of his leadership style cause too many mistakes or general resistance to change.

True leadership is the persistence in skill building and acknowledging of errors. Remember, a leader's credibility is meeting others' needs before their own and working to be of service.

To summarize, all of us have blended styles and different intensities. These influences are telling us what we like and dislike. In other words, what we prefer and do not prefer, and how we'll interact with life is influenced by our style.

- So as a leader, how do you show up?

- Do you bring a hammer to a workplace that requires a saw?

- Are you conscious and congruent in your natural leadership style, allowing your preferences and patterns to emerge?

- Do you listen to feedback from others about how you can increase your credibility?

- Can you shift your leadership style to get the results that you want?

- Can you take responsibility, not to change your style, but alter your interaction with others, in the work environment, to get results?

I've mentioned in previous chapters that leaders must be consistent and credible to be effective. If your personal leadership style is not building credibility, then you are responsible for changing your approach, to achieve what you want. Skilled leaders understand this. We're not asking you to be different or change your entire approach, just to be flexible in any given moment.

LEADERSHIP IS NOT FOR WIMPS

Now one of the things I want to emphasize is that your leadership style does not predict your success. It doesn't inherently determine your flexibility to work with others. Leadership style only says, "Here are my preferences." So all leadership styles, at one time or another, have been represented as being successful within the context of life and sports. So yes, there are some that have natural tendencies and are easier to flow into it.

Erroneous thinking would say that you couldn't be a leader because of your personal style. That doesn't reflect that you're willing develop the skill sets. So we don't want to look at these styles in a judgmental way. We want to use our leadership styles as a basis for developing strengths, competence, and interactions.

LEADING WITH HEART AND SOUL

I always say that the job of a long snapper in the NFL was one of service. My job was not long snapper; my job was service, and I put my heart and soul in every snap, day in and day out for fifteen years.

CEO Ken Keis continues the task of bringing heart and soul into leadership behavior and skill building. This is independent and in addition to your leadership style:

☑ **Heart** is the emotional or moral as distinguished from the intellectual nature. A leader with heart is distinguished by one's innermost character, feelings, or inclinations.

☑ **Soul** is the animating principle, or actuating cause of an individual life; the spiritual principle embodied in human beings is usually observed as a leader with a purpose, a specific mission.

I snapped the ball back to the holder so that the kicker could do his job, which was to put the ball through the uprights for three points. For me, it wasn't enough to get the ball back there accurately. No, I made sure that the laces were facing out when the holder caught the ball so that the ball did not have to be spun. The last thing the kicker wants to see is a ball spinning, or worse yet, one with the laces facing him.

The ball I snap to the holder eight yards behind me rotates exactly three and a half times before the holder catches it. The laces are pointing out, and he simply sets it down. In addition, I locate the ball right over the spot that it will be put down so that the action happens more quickly. This allows the kicker more time to see the ball and increases his chances at success.

It is that attitude that carries over into my business

and personal life. My leadership role within any organization is about service. If I do my job, you never hear my name. It's not about me; it's about the success of the play and the three points that go up on the scoreboard.

I still find opportunities to lead. Often when we're kicking a field goal, it's because we were stopped on the third down. There can be a natural let down for those players who were on offense because of their perceived failure to score a touchdown. If I sense this, I start talking to those in the huddle that we're not getting three instead of six, but rather three instead of zero. I want them to realize the gravity of the play, that it's still important and more than likely will make a difference in the game. It is always perception versus reality. The perception to some might be that we failed because we didn't score a touchdown. The reality is the outcome could be decided on whether we get three or zero.

●●●

Keis:

"What is missing from many businesses and organizations today is heart and soul. Would you like it if people called you and your organization heartless or soulless? Of course not! But, if you don't intentionally include heart and soul as foundational principles—vital to your success—you are committing the sin of omission.

"Who cares if we have it together mentally and

physically, if there's no heart and soul? Just last month, another survey conducted by Global TV verified that over 50% of working individuals are not at all engaged at their work.

"The reality is that in the majority of organizations, HR departments and career professionals currently are not assisting the majority of people to be connected to their profession or job. Where is our heart and soul when we continue to support and perpetuate dissatisfaction and lack of engagement at work?

"We all would agree that fully engaged and on purpose employees and players have far more potential to contribute than those who are not. Why are we not acting on that challenge?

"Here are some reasons people don't lead with heart and soul, personally and professionally:

"Fear of the unknown and the potential outcome. Because so few organizations function at top levels, then soulful leadership and performance can appear an overwhelming task or project. They could worry, "What if this approach goes sideways and reduces results?" They are usually driven by a lack of confidence or competence.

"A sign of weakness - Professionals have said to me that service-oriented leadership is a sign of weakness. The book *Good To Great* (HarperCollins, 2001) confirmed that great leaders care about their people and demonstrate humility in the process. Operating with heart and soul actually displays confidence and strength in your convictions.

CONCLUSION

I appreciate greatly Keis' insights after years of working and researching how leaders can influence and serve in the most effective manner. As Ken reminds us, "to lead others with heart and soul, you first must set a good example. Credibility will come from what you are doing—not from what you are saying." I could say it no better.

"To lead from the heart requires that you and others are connected to your respective purpose."

Ken Keis, CEO, Consulting Resource Group

CHAPTER FOUR

Influential Leaders

"The truth is that, given the right environment and
culture, most individuals want to contribute and
communicate at the heart and soul level. We simply
have not given them the chance or supported a culture
that personally or organizationally embraces it!"

Ken Keis, CEO, Consulting Resource Group

INFLUENCE

Think for a moment about a person who influenced
your life. You might remember the teacher who
took an interest in you and encouraged your
performance. Their ability to influence was through
your relationship. You might think of Mother Teresa,
whom we admire because of her selfless service. Her
ability to influence was through her charismatic
actions. The tech world recognizes the young
genius, Mark Zuckerberg, founder of Facebook, as

the current, most influential person in high-tech industry. His ability to influence others is through his expertise and his ability to manifest his vision.

People who influence you take time to develop relationships, have earned your trust, or mentor you because of their expertise, skills, or service. Leaders influence you through their styles as well as ability to relate through several avenues that pertain to a need, desire, or a trigger within you that makes you listen.

- Your desire to achieve
- Your desire to be challenged, awakened, and improved
- Your need to learn and improve competencies
- Your desire to be engaged, mentored, and supporter through relationship
- You see the vision, feel the strength, and join the team
- You hear the message and desire the transformation

Punishment, coercion, and abusive authoritarian tactics, which most leaders of this new century consider bullying and demeaning, can also motivate us. These tactics only produce short-term results and such influence is based on fears and negativity. There is no long-term result, but the long-term effect of coercion, whether in business, parenting, or NFL leadership is damage to the personalities involved.

Positive and effective influence is built on credible relationships of constructive benefit to all. Rapport is built, trust is established, and the character values are compatible.

Within the NFL, as in the game of life, people of positive influence, that is people of heart and soul, know how to inspire us and help us perfect our skills and talents. We speak of the NFL influencers as legends because they endure the wins and losses, the adverse media, the travel and time away from family. Legends endure.

LEGENDS IN OUR OWN TIME

Morten Andersen knows that coach Dan Reeves is a powerful leader. "I had certainly had the most success with him. We also had a team of great players, and Reeves facilitated their competence in an environment that inspired us all. He could be charismatic."

While Dan Reeves was best remembered for his coaching, this quarterback was inducted into the Hall of Fame of his alma mater, the University of South Carolina, in 1977. He spent his entire career as a player with the Dallas Cowboys. However, that career was cut short by injuries. Appreciated for his leadership skills, his coaching career also began with the Dallas Cowboys, where he first coached running backs and was later promoted to offensive coordinator. In 1981, Reeves became the youngest head coach in the league by taking that position for the Denver Broncos, where he stayed for the next twelve years. In 1993, Reeves became head coach of the Giants and in 1996, of the Atlanta Falcons. He finally left the game of football in 2003.

Another NFL influencer was Bum Phillips, as Mort Andersen describes him.

Anderson:

"Bum Philips also was an influential leader. Bum sold the family unit; that's what he believed in. The team was a family. You really felt that there were fifty-three brothers together in this game. Bum sold that successfully. He would come into team meetings, and you would think he was going to talk about the game that we had just played or the game coming up. Yet he didn't. For thirty minutes, he'd spend time talking about financial preparation and how we should invest. You know, he would give life lessons. He's been trying to make you a better person, not just a better football player.

"That really proved to me he was more concerned about you as a person and your success in life. Then if you succeeded in life, you would succeed in football. Phillips always said that football would give you more than you could give football. I certainly agree with that. But also that football was just a small part of your life, and that you have to realize this game will outlast everybody. He made sure we had a good foundation. He would bring people in that were experts in other fields and talk to us about all kinds of things in life. For a young player like me, twenty-

GAME PLAN

two-year's old, it was a revelation, a tremendous help to me to start my career with a coach like that. He was fun to play for. He really wanted to win football because he invested so much time in preparing you and it was wonderful."

In the 1950s and 60s, Bum Phillips coached high school football in several Texas towns. His early college coaching years were as an assistant coach for universities like Southern Methodist University, Texas A&M, Oklahoma State University, and several others. In the early 1970s, Sid Gillman hired Phillips as a defensive coach for the San Diego Chargers, and this opened the door to his NFL coaching career. Described as folksy and humans, Phillips moved to the Houston Oilers as defensive coordinator when Gillman became the Oilers' head coach, and then replaced Gillman in that position in 1975. From 1981 through the 1985 season, Phillips was the head coach for Saints. After retirement, he worked as a football analyst for television and radio.

Jack Del Rio was also influence by Bum Phillips, his very first coach. Del Rio shared that Bum was tremendous and impressed upon him the value and importance of family and doing the right thing as a man.

Many players consider Coach Ditka to be a personable mentor. Danny Wuerffel describes Coach Ditka as generous to people, and loyal to his team and players, perhaps even to a fault. As a coach,

73

players like Wuerffel wanted to work hard and not disappoint Ditka, as did I when I played for the Saints. Bobby April speaks of Ditka as a charismatic coach.

April:

"Mike Ditka had an amazing record playing for the Bears. Ditka earned the title of Rookie of the Year and continued with the Bears for five seasons, each one including a Pro Bowl game. After playing for the Cowboys and Eagles, Ditka retired and moved into coaching.

"His first position was assistant coach under Tom Landry with the Cowboys. Known as "Iron Mike" or "Da Coach," Ditka's NFL coaching career then moved to the position of head coach for the Chicago Bears, including a Super Bowl win in 1985, as well as a three-year stint with the New Orleans Saints. His time with the Bears also won him the title of NFL Coach of the Year in 1985 and 1988. Ditka has also been a sports broadcaster and appeared in cameo spots on several television shows.

"I think Coach Ditka loved the NFL and loved the league. I learned from Coach Ditka, as did many others. He was humble about his opportunities in his career; I mean he was thankful. You don't think that a guy of his stature would think like that.

"And he's one of the signature guys in the league. If somebody said 'Name ten players, great players in from the last generation,' Ditka would definitely be one of them. I realized that he loved the game, the game was great to him and that he owed a lot to the game.

"He did not take the game for granted, he felt it was an honor to go out and represent this league wearing an NFL uniform. To be around that attitude everyday for three years makes me always try to relay that same message. Ditka would say, 'don't take it for granted, man. This is real honor to be able to do what you've chosen to do.'

"He always reminded us that nobody was bigger than the game. The game was here long before we got into it, and the game will be here long after we get out of it. I think that's always resonated with me, and I think you can carry that over into the business world. If any one person thinks they're bigger than the whole, they are not because it takes the effort of the team. With team success comes individual accolades."

THE TEAM

Absolutely, every team member benefits when the team wins. Some guys will receive tremendous rewards for their team's success. I once heard a player make this statement: *The real star of the team is the whole team.*

To play on any team, whether corporate, sports, or family is not a right, but a privilege. The privilege involves the passions and pride in contributing to your team and benefiting from the synergy and enthusiasm. For example, although a lot of coaches are tremendous, Ditka exemplified the tremendous passion for the game. Of all the coaches I worked with, Ditka had a way of talking about the league that made everybody feel like we're lucky to be here and we ought to give it all that we have because we owe it our best. Bobby April also experienced Ditka's generosity.

April:

"Unbelievable" was the only way you could put his generosity. I remember a time this church group was having a golf tournament to raise money for the church. For a donation of $50, they'd put your name by a golf hole. I went to Ditka and said, 'Coach, I know this is probably a pain in the neck, but what do you think about donating to this deal?' Well, Ditka looked at the figure, whipped out a checkbook and wrote a $500 donation.

"It was Coach Ditka's policy to buy lunch for the entire staff throughout the entire off-season. I'd been out with Ditka and we had Po-boys down in Chalmette at Rocky and Carlos, a famous establishment down river from New Orleans where I lived when I played for the Saints. We brought the whole staff over there with Coach Ditka, and he ended up tipping the waitresses about $300. The story goes that the family emigrated from Italy and settled into this one neighborhood, bought the restaurant, and went into business. Some of the ladies still spoke no English. But when the generous Ditka tipped them, one lady was very emotional and filled with gratitude and expressed it in Italian.

"Ditka often reminded his players of the old country in his conservatism and in habits, like carrying a big wad of cash, and he put rubber bands around it. He'd undo those rubber bands and flip those $100 bills and give them to the people. He wanted to give back. He knows that he's been blessed in many ways, and he wants to share it."

The subject of Ditka also reminds me of someone who has influenced many people in the NFL, and that person is Jack Del Rio. I relay this story about Jack because I think he's a unique guy, and his story is distinctive. Jack didn't have a very long career in coaching before he got to be a head coach. This story goes back to earlier years when Jack was with the Saints; and we were teammates.

Initially, Coach Ditka brought Jack on board the Saints; I don't know if the organization was going to make any spot for him because Jack had been out of football, working for a year. Jack had complete confidence that he was ready to coach. He outlined his plan to become a head coach in the near future, five years as I remember it, one afternoon while we were working out. Now, coming from someone else, this might have seemed somewhat brash, and maybe it was. But to me, I saw a man with a plan to get where he wanted to go. I observed in Jack a person with a keen awareness of who he was and what he felt he was capable of accomplishing. What I observed in our time together with the Saints was how completely confidant he grew when he set his goals and aimed for his star.

Del Rio embodied self-confidence and inspired everyone around him. Coach Ditka knew that this guy could coach, and he hired him as an assistant.

People recognized his skills and intelligence as a coordinator. He reeked of confidence that rallied people to his cause. Yet, Del Rio also feels that Minnesota Vikings defensive coordinator Tony Dungy's leadership style brought out the best he's ever played.

Tony Dungy's NFL career started as a free agent with the Pittsburgh Steelers, and he had a Super Bowl championship in the 1978 season. In 1979, he played for the 49ers and then the New York Giants where his NFL career ended. His coaching career started at his alma mater, The University of Minnesota, in 1980, as assistant coach. In 1981, he became an assistant coach for the Steelers, and then moved on as defensive coordinator for the Chiefs, and eventually the Vikings. His first head coaching opportunity came with the Tampa Bay Buccaneers, where he established his reputation as a winning coach. He then moved onto the Indianapolis Colts where a long career was rewarded with a Super Bowl XLI championship on February 4, 2007. I have only met Coach Dungy briefly, but what I had heard of him was confirmed in my short experience with him. Simply put, he is genuine and kind. I contend that he is one of a kind in the NFL coaching profession. His book, *Quiet Strength* (Group Publishing, Inc, 2007), is a captivating must-read in my opinion.

Del Rio:

"I went to Minnesota and I played for Tony Dungy, my defensive coordinator. Monty Kiffin was the linebacker coach. Together, they embraced what I could do as a player and sought to eliminate any gray area. They made things black and white, and I appreciated that as an intelligent football player. I liked the detail of studying an opponent. Being able to play fast was something that they taught and emphasized, and so I blossomed there. I played my best football for Tony there in Minnesota.

"He commands an ultimate amount of respect for as soft spoken as he is. Tony has his own style. He doesn't raise his voice very often, doesn't use foul language. Yet, he has strong conviction, and you understand very clearly what he's looking for in a player or in a game.

"He's a coach that you very much want to please because of the quality that he represents. He's such a classy guy, but I think what I drew out of my experience with Tony was that he is a rock, a solid person.

"What I drew from him that I utilize myself now, as a coach, is to eliminate the gray. Many coaches will have a plan, and then when the other team has a good play, try and tell you that you should have done something differently even though you did exactly what you were coached to do, and it was a good play against you.

"Tony was the first coach who would say, 'That was a heck of a play by them. Let's tackle that and let's go to the next one.' He wouldn't try and make his defensive scheme look like it was perfect and that the player was wrong. He would admit that they had a good play, talk about the need to get the guy on the ground, and then let's go to the next play. As long as you were giving him the technique he was looking for, he would never turn on you.

"Tony was consistently willing to admit when the other coach had a good scheme against us, and I believe in that. I believe as a coach it's important that we say, 'Hey they got us. That was good design on their part, and you did exactly what I asked you to do, and you did it exactly right.'"

CONCLUSION

On your road to leadership, remember those who helped you along the way. Don't forget to turn around and help those who admire you. This is a good way to ensure service-oriented leadership in the next generations.

CHAPTER FIVE

Got a Game Plan?

A dream is just a dream.
A goal is a dream with a plan and a deadline.

Harvey Mackay

INTRODUCTION

A *Game Plan* is the road map for how a leader accomplishes his or her work, mission, task, or meeting. In order to have a game plan, a leader has the answer to the big question of "why," such as *why am I here* and *why am I doing this*? When we can answer the big "why" for ourselves, we find the inner motivation to complete our work or play, be present in relationships, and move through our days with unbridled passion. I can say with assurance that everyone I have met in the NFL knew their answers to the big why, and I'll explain this in the section called Three Motivating Values. Your answer to the why question will be your motivation!

NFL players and coaches find their motivation through their physical intelligence for the sport, a passion for the planning and plays, a great salary for their skills, or the brotherhood of the game. For you, the external motivators fall into place when you know why you do what you do.

As you learned in the last chapter, each personal leadership style correlates to a motivational style.

- A behavioral style leader aims to achieve.

- A cognitive analyzer loves to learn.

- An interpersonal harmonizer uses compassion to foster caring.

- An affective-style leader intends to influence.

From recognizing your main style or the style blends that best suit your leadership, you can incorporate self-motivating techniques into your game plan.

In this book, we've discussed the service of leadership and putting the heart and soul back into leadership. I've learned that my leadership style stems from my values of being in service to others, whether my coach, team member, sons, or wife. I have a blended leadership style. As an interpersonal, I work to be of service, my primary value. As a behavioral achiever, I love to win and I will practice to achieve that goal. As an affective leader, I am now finding enjoyment in influencing others like high school students when I give a talk or attend a youth conference, address CEOs at a business conference, or inspire my sons to be better people.

Clarifying your values is a key step to ensuring that you spend your time and energy on those things that are most important to your game plan. Knowing your leadership style can guide your values, and values are paramount to your motivation.

THREE MOTIVATING VALUES

I've observed that three motivators exist for most players in professional football, based upon their personal values, which is their love of money, family, and the game itself. These motivators empower players to withstand the NFL pressures. After all, football-filled nights require top-notch leadership skills.

There are games on Sunday afternoons, Sunday nights, Monday nights, and Thursday nights in midseason. We even play on Saturdays once college football season goes into hibernation until their bowl games. There is no doubt that America is in love with NFL football, which can be a glamorous occupation. With glamour often come the spoils. So why do players play?

- For the love of money
- For the love of family
- For the love of the game

"Love of money" is a realization of how much is on the line financially. Any given NFL player knows his performance dictates whether he gets the chance to "front" or to acquire the proverbial bling. It's unfortunate if this is the lone motivating value that drives a player. When shows like *MTV Cribs* perpetuate the glamour of sports stars in their big homes with their nice cars or other "big boy toys," the glamour is short-lived. The fun lasts a brief time, and the same player, without internal values to motivate his game plan, seeks the next bout of glamour.

In my last off-season I was asked to give a tour of my home for a local show. I initially accepted, but later declined after talking it over with my wife. We felt like it wasn't the right thing for us, to set a good example for our two boys. We talk to them often about how fortunate we are to have some of the things we have. We continue this with the thought that we enjoy what we have, not only with ourselves, but also with others as often as possible. We attempt to finalize the thought process with the fact that you don't ever boast to others about material possessions.

So the value of achieving for the "love of money"

works well when it stems from your internal value and drive for success in the game of football or business. But the "bling" eventually fades on almost everything. I remember Coach Mike Ditka saying how the money would come, and that's great, but it will also eventually go. There has to be something else. In his opinion, the memories and friendships were long lasting.

"Love of family" is felt more by the veteran players. They've been in the league for three or more seasons and have started their families. They come to realize that the NFL is their livelihood, the value of which now supports their families. This was certainly my case as I entered my fifth year in the league. I made the final cut on Monday, but was then released Monday evening. My wife Leslie was six weeks away from giving birth. The anxiety I felt coming home from Three Rivers Stadium after being cut is a moment I'll never forget. The value of our families provides heartfelt motivation for parents, coaches, and business people every day.

"Love of the game" is a self-induced pressure or self-motivating value. "For the love of the game" is the expectation of the individual to perform because he can't accept failure. The player has a realization that what is expected of him helps the common goal of the team.

We can see this in our families when a young child wants to help with dinner or raking the leaves. This internal pride of performing at a certain level for the team, the family, or the business is the greatest type of motivating force. On of my favorite Vermeil quotes is this, "What's the difference between a young rookie and a true pro? A young rookie works hard to learn how to do it right. A true pro works hard so he never does it wrong." The second part sums up the thought. A true pro works hard so he never does it wrong, not because he wants a nice car. Hey, if the car comes in the package, then the leader has a bigger win!

I think these three values motivate all of us. Enjoy the spoils, support your family, and have true respect for your game. These defined values provide you with enough desire to perform at the required levels because you ultimately want to win! Skilled leaders who recognize their personal styles know the answer to the big question of why? Why do they follow their passion? Why are they motivated each morning to persist in their work?

THE GAME PLAN

Why do you lead in the way that you do? Now that you have recognized your personal style of leadership and those values that motivate your actions, you can accomplish whatever you desire through your game plan. A game plan consists of your goals, your action steps, and your accountability.

STYLES...VALUES...GOALS...ACTIONS...ACCOUNTABILITY

In the game plan for your success are these assets...

- ✓ Values define your styles.
- ✓ Your style shapes your actions.
- ✓ Your goal is the destination for your journey.
- ✓ Your actions are the means to get you to the goal.
- ✓ Accountability is the integrity of how you get there.

GOALS

Goals are positive in nature and reflect what you are moving toward. The motion toward an achievement that you value drives your actions. Goals are derived from, and thus are consistent with your values. When I set my goals for my game plan, I focus on five questions:

1. What will I do?

2. How long will it take?

3. What is involved?

4. What effort will it take?

5. What benefit will I receive?

Notice that I build my motivation right into the goal as my benefit. I suggest your goals be ambitious, as well as specific. Specific goals are measurable. You can answer the questions, "How will I know when I've achieved my goal. What do the results look like?" For instance, when my sons and I discuss the goal of cleaning their room, I might say the result is "all the toys and clothes are cleared from the floor and furniture." They could stuff clothes and clutter under their beds and meet the goal of "cleared from the floor." To leave no doubt about my expectations in our goal setting, I will add these results: hang up clothes, restore shoes to closets, and put books on bookshelves." The results are clear, and my sons can easily achieve them, feeling the sense of accomplishment and contribution.

When the results of your goals are clear and measurable, they are achievable within a specific time frame. Avoid goals that are based in an activity. Saying, "I will exercise daily," may not be clear enough to motivate you. If you say, "I will do strength training at nine o'clock each morning," then your mind has a time anchor, and you'll be watching the clock and being accountable. Like I do, make a list of the benefits to you!

Understand that outcome-based goals bring success, and activity-based goals produce a lot of activity, usually without completion or success. People who have written goals are much more successful than those who do not have written goals. In my experiences with Coach Vermeil, I have watched him practice goal setting, and asked him to share his thoughts with you.

Vermeil:

"My goals always tie in with my vision. I've used long-range goals in my coaching years. The busier I have become, I've gone from longer-range goals to daily objectives, things we have to do today, tomorrow, the next day. I write them down and I check them off.

"I have learned more by writing objectives down than by thinking about long-range goals. You think about the results when you start writing them down, trying to put it so other people are going to read and understand them. Then the coaching staff and the organization members understand the purpose and activity.

"I always need to be looking forward in terms of what I'm working at. That tends to drive me in my day-to-day activities, like using the daily planner.

"Every day I used to fill out two pages because I wrote down notes on conversations that I have. Say I had ten different conversations with different players. I'd summarize briefly in my daily planner what that conversation was about, the outcomes, or other notes. Otherwise I tend to forget. Still the first thing in the morning comes down to my daily planner and see, number 1, number 2, number 3 phones calls to make."

It is that commitment to the goal and the discipline to take the necessary steps that make the difference. Mort Andersen tells us:

Andersen:

"I do have goals, and I do write them down. I write them down every year and some of them remain the same. Others have changed as I've gone through my career. I think goals need to be motivational, specific, and realistic. Goals are your personal tools to get to the place you want to go. It's kind of like a GPS to provide your road map, a direct route around traffic, if you will.

"I set my goals so they are non-threatening. I'll give you an example. Let's say I want to make 100 percent of my field goals. Well, what happens if I miss a field goal? Does that mean the rest of my season is a failure? What I learned to do was set 'goal windows.' These goal windows are the percentages that I could live with if I only made 80 or 85 percent of my goal. Goal windows are standards or percentages I can live with. If I made 80 to 85 percent of my field goals, that's a successful year.

ACTION

Action is the second level of a game plan, after well-defined goals. I like Andersen's goal windows strategy, because it provides for the action of challenging himself to move to the next step. Planning in detail the steps necessary to achieve your goals makes them real, gives them more credibility than mere intentions. Action plans "actualize" goals. Goals tell you where you want to go. Action plans tell you what you must do to ensure you get there.

- Identify the steps necessary to achieve your goal.

- Determine if they are sequential. If not, then make parallel lists of necessary steps.

- Add completion times for each step to maintain an accountability system.

- Goals and actions plans are dynamic, not static. Change them often to accommodate the challenges and opportunities you encounter.

A game plan of goals, actions, and measurements provides you with a system for success, for achievement, and for expectations. The system allows for clear communication and understanding among team members, family members, and business partners.

ACCOUNTABILITY

Accountability is the third step of the game plan, and refers to taking responsibility for bringing your game plan goals to fruition. You may do this well, or you might desire the help of an accountability partner. When I set my goals, I make myself accountable to my coach, my wife, or teammate, depending upon the setting and context. In doing so, I am responsible for completing my game plan goals, yet I raise the stakes when I have a partner who cheers me in the process. Consider the idea of an accountability partner if you find follow-through difficult.

Here is Bobby April's take on accountability.

April:

"My ultimate goal is to be a head coach as well. In that leadership position, I feel motivated by the team factors, people whom I'm accountable to. The team motives are concerns for their contributions to the team, and then to the organizational achievement. That's an honorable goal to be accountable by saying, 'Hey I'm going to help make a very prestigious organization better.'

"The accountability challenge is overcoming the obstacles to working to fulfilling your potential. That's a tremendous motive. "

Accountability contains two strong values: personal responsibility and choice.

Accountability starts with you, a leader who owns the value of personal responsibility for making your game plan happen. Personal responsibility is an affirming choice. In your day-to-day life, managing your plan for success, you might establish an accountability review. Like Vermeil, you might check off your objectives each hour. If you find unaccomplished goals about three months into your game plan, you don't blame or guilt-trip yourself. Rather, you define new milestones, breaking them into easily accomplished steps.

On a larger scale, the leaders described in this book emphasize personal responsibility as a team contributor. A personally responsible leader is a straight shooter for his team. He calls a spade a spade without casting blame and he is open-minded. If game plans fail, then accountability calls for new realizations to change the direction of the game plan. Reorganize the goals, and point to achievement in a different direction. Accountability calls for a leader to "handle" the failures as well as the wins. Here is Andersen's input.

Andersen:

"Personal responsibility is important in leadership roles. You will be asked to walk the walk and take responsibility for mistakes that you make whether they are actually yours or not. You may be called on to take one on the chin for the team. Being a leader may mean saying, 'Hey, it was on me because I'm ultimately responsible for the rest of the team.' I think that's very big if you can do that. If you're willing to redirect blame and responsibility for a mistake on to you, that frees up other people to continue contributing successfully to the team. It really shows a lot of character, integrity, and mental toughness. When a leader can take personal responsibility in tough situations, he's a true team player."

When we choose to be accountable within our game plan, our personal choices become as important as our actions. As Coach Vermeil reiterated, "The power of choice is the greatest power we all have." This point is illustrated in his story.

Vermeil:

"I went through an experience a week ago when listening to my brother present the eulogy for his thirty-two year old son who committed suicide. My brother spoke about enjoying the years he had with his son and through the eulogy he was helping those around him make a choice about remembering the great points in his son's life. He was setting the tone for how he wanted other people to respond and act, and help each other.

"The funeral reminded me that each day, each moment, we make those choices. I've watched people get into the habit of making bad choices. What you allow to enter your mind is even a choice. As you know, some kids today were in environments that didn't offer many opportunities to make the good choice."

Your power of choosing becomes a habit. Your choices become your actions, and you are accountable for these.

Vermeil:

"My job as a head coach was being able to read people and see what they're about, where they came from, how they are, and then being genuinely interested in them as a person. I made my choice as to help my assistant coaches do everything better than they've ever done it before.

"My job with my players is to take a player individually and help him choose to be better than he's ever been. Then when you collectively build your team, each member can improve 2 percent, and that's a huge, huge jump in overall team performance."

CONCLUSION

Join the inspiring leaders in families, business, and sports by developing and achieving a successful game plan. The steps are:

Styles...Values...Goals...Action...Accountability

Through determining your unique or blended personal style, you'll know what talents and gifts you bring to the game plan. You find your motivation to achieve your goals and develop your game plan through what you value and strongly believe in. It could be family values, monetary well-being, or the joy of the game itself.

Your goals are the light at the end of your tunnel, and the action plan is how you move through the tunnel. Some people zip through; others enjoy a more measured program for achievement. To be a leader, you must know you can, and then take action and be accountable for the steps you take. They'll lead you to the top!

CHAPTER SIX

Forging a Team

The quality of a person's life is in direct proportion
to their commitment to excellence, regardless of their
chosen field of endeavor.

Vince Lombardi

TEAMS VERSUS GROUPS

A great group of rookies with outstanding skills
comes together to play, but they are not yet a team.
Groups become effective teams by moving through
specific bonding, organizing and creating dialogue
to shape their skills. Within every effective group,
people come together to achieve a goal, participate
in a vision, or join forces for accomplishment of a
common task. This is a team!

Members' earnest participation and contributions
create synergy—a synchronization of efforts that
produces a greater result than the combined efforts

of the single members. It is what is meant by the whole being greater than the sum of its parts.

GOOD LEADERSHIP BUILDS A TEAM

What do you think unites a team, makes a team come together and be able to cooperatively merge their efforts? Our contributors offer their views first.

Mawae:

"Building the team and being a team member starts with the coach or the leader. The leader, as a team member, is also a follower. I think ultimately you have to have a vision of where you want to go, and then, you've got to be able to communicate that vision in a clear and concise manner so your team will understand it. Your team has to buy in to it, then they want your vision to become their vision."

April:

"For team building, you create morale and create synergy where all the members are working together. You have to create it as a leader; that's your job. Yes, creating the synergy of everybody working together is definitely the leader's number one job.

"In any profession, when a leader is hired, their job description should always include these qualities.

1. Communicating with team members

2. Recognizing problems

3. Addressing those problems

4. Having empathy

5. Having the intuition"

Keis:

"In team building, whether in sports or businesses, a leader works from peoples' personal styles and strengths. Always identify certain strengths and specific skills as the member's contributions to the team. A leader has the ability to bring together people who have complementary strengths, which is a critical process and a benchmark of successful leadership. Team members could be of complementary personal styles or be individuals who are opposite of the leader in style."

HOW TO WIN WITH A GREAT TEAM

Let me introduce you to Frank Gansz, Jr., one of my coaches for four years with the Kansas City Chiefs. Ganz, Jr. was the special teams coach for the Chiefs from 2001 to 2005. Before that, he spent three seasons with the Raiders, and after, two with the Ravens. Presently he is the coordinator for special teams at UCLA. Ganz, Jr. has a game plan for a winning team! What Frank talks of and preaches on a daily basis is this: You must know what it is you are to do.

1. **Assignment** - Simply put, what is expected of you becomes your job or assignment.

2. **Alignment** - How you get ready for the assignment, whether it is running down a

football field or giving a presentation in the boardroom, is your alignment. Often times, if one isn't prepared properly, the success is compromised from the start. Football is about leverage and angles. You can have all the talent in the world, but if you've lined up wrong, you may possibly give an inferior opponent an advantage, which could be difficult, or even impossible, to overcome.

3. **Technique** - Technique amounts to how you are going to do your assignment. As I snap a ball between my legs, there are certain steps I know I have to perform in order for the snap, and ultimately the play, to be successful. It's really no different in business. You know how something must be presented to give you the best possible chance at success.

4. **Execution** - Execution refers to the actual process. As football players, we work all week at the prior traits. We understand what it is we need to do. We then study what is the best possible position to be in against our opponent, and what it is we will do specifically to be successful.

5. **Finish** - Ultimately, it then comes down to execution and finish. Do we do what we set out to do in the best possible manner, and then more importantly, do we finish?

In football terms, finish is often talked about in tackling terms—wrapping your arms up, driving your legs, and getting the person down to the ground. The "finish" in business might be as simple as the hand written thank- you note, or as involved as the counterproposal. Your plan may be going as you mapped it out from day one over a year ago, but unless you execute it properly and finish what was started, you'll never reach your goal.

COLLABORATIVE EFFORTS BUILD GREAT TEAMS

Team building begins when family members come together for a meeting about household rules or a business team is ready for project collaboration. In football, team building could be rookies who are ready to learn their positions and play as a group. Specific steps help define group dynamics. In the broadest sense, a team is characterized by their feeling of belonging to or participating in something greater than themselves. Next, the coach or leader is responsible for fostering and designing the experience of a team for effective results. For example, in sports, coaches focus on service, which is helping their players become better people as well as players.

Mawae:

"I think the ultimate epitome of a leader was Christ because he brought himself below everybody to serve him or her. "I once heard a speech in which the speaker referred to the fact that if you have a towel, you can do two things with it. You can sit there and waive the towel like a rally flag, or you can wrap it around your waist and be a waiter. The point was being willing to serve people and to serve their needs. Others look at those actions and attitudes.

"I know many good people who want to make it right for others. When you realize that you're a part of something bigger than yourself, then that gives you the ability and the attitude to step down and say, 'This isn't for me. This is for them or for those that come after us.' I think that's what people buy into, and when they see that, then they allow you to be the leader that you already know you can be."

Keis:

"Building a winning team is not about being nice; it is about being consistent and fair. This is where courage comes into play. It takes courage to hold individuals accountable, but the alternative is disrespectful to the rest of the team—and is certainly not reflective of successful leadership.

"When team members are not measuring up, you have only three choices:

- Get them to change their attitude and behavior;
- Accept their behavior and lower your expectations

to match their poor performance; or

- Replace those individuals.

"If you want to build a winning team, there are no other options. Well-meaning and nice team members who are not ready or able to perform their duties are, in many ways, the most difficult people to lead because their commitment is high but their abilities are not.

"Aligning personal style with the work/job style of a position is critical for success, but that comes after you ensure that the individual has the talent and the ability to fulfill the job's responsibilities. For example: I have a talent for business and public speaking, but please don't ask me to fix your car. I can do a basic oil change, but I don't have car expertise above that level. No matter how hard I try, I will never have the talent to be a mechanic! That is true for all your team members. So while we all have natural talents and acquired skills, it is essential that they match the needs of the organization in which we work."

•••

DEVELOPING AN EFFECTIVE AND PHENOMENAL TEAM

In the book, *The ABC's of Building a Business Team That Wins* (Business Plus, 2004), author Blair Singer, lists six qualities of a team player.

1. Energy

2. Unstoppable desire to win

3. Willingness to let someone else win

4. Taking personal responsibility

5. Willingness to submit to the "code"

6. Offering their unique talent

In this case, Singer defines the code as a "set of simple, powerful rules that govern the internal behavior of any team, organization or family, individual or even nation."[ii] Singer refers to the code as a way to check your internal values as compared to the team values. They have to be in sync and aligned.

When a team is losing, what factor causes their last minute push to win? What internal resilience brings families together in times of distress? To me, it's one's moral compass. Singer calls it the code, the internal rules, which determine how we behave toward one another and be accountable for those actions. In this book, our code exemplifies similar components.

- Leadership in service
- The heart and soul of respect
- Empathy
- Appreciation for our team members

In any team dynamics, the rapport-building steps for effective results are common among most groups.

1. The leader clarifies the team vision, explains the family plan or the parameters of the business goal, remembering that the team members exist to support the team.

2. Team members identify their talents, strengths, and contributions to the game plan. This is accomplished through personal style inventories or self-assessment. The leader knows their traits, and through discussion helps team members define their roles and contributions. This is a requisite if you are to avoid disruption from those personalities that don't quite mesh with the rest of the team.

3. A skilled leader, having identified personal styles of team members, sets the stage for commonality of skills. Is everyone willing to speak up? Does everyone agree never to assume, but to ask? Are there specific behavioral boundaries to be respected? Is everyone comfortable receiving feedback? Obviously these team-building ground rules will differ

for an executive team or a family with young children. However, the same code process applies to any group.

4. Team members practice, perform, and receive immediate, positive feedback. Feedback should be extensive, not only from the leader, but from other team members as well. Practicing informal communication outside of the designated meeting times also keeps communication channels open.

5. The NFL, a business, or a family create their own culture, and the team functions within this culture. Leaders make mistakes if they assume that all family or team members agree with or will abide by those cultural rules. Cohesion results from reinforcing the results you want to achieve. Utilize appreciation, recognition, and rewards to reinforce the code. Celebrate success and share the fun of winning.

Coaches want to establish specific leadership patterns in their teams, just like a manager brings to his team or a parent defines for a family.

☑ We are in this together! Every member of the team or family adds value and talents.

☑ We have to pull together to achieve the goals. Each contributor's efforts create greater momentum for the team.

☑ We challenge each other. Team members learn by stretching to meet their goal, working harder to respond to the challenge to be more and to be better.

☑ We consistently compete everyday. Team members compete with themselves first, and then each other to practice and perfect their skills.

BEING A GREAT TEAM CONTRIBUTOR

Ken Keis has said that, "In my primary research for my MBA, the number one factor affecting an individual's job satisfaction, morale, and productivity was found to be the person to whom the individual directly reports." This is so true in a family, corporation, and especially on an NFL team. The parent, the boss, or the coach have that undeniable influence and the ability to inspire. This is the privilege of being such a leader, the ability to be of service. I think Coach Vermeil's guidelines for leading and building a team summarize this process through common-sense leadership guidelines for teams.

Vermeil:

"I spoke to the Ritz Carlton chain, the whole organization in Chicago Wednesday morning for an hour, and I have a leadership preparation approach that I followed as a coach in my organizations. They are so simple that I call them seven common-sense principles of leadership because common sense is not always a common practice.

"In leadership you can see and you can hear people do the dumbest things while working with each other, and they're not even aware they're doing it. To me, you've got to surround yourself with people that like other people, care about people, and you as a leader have to care about people. This philosophy is reflected in the common-sense guidelines.

1. Players or team members don't care how much you know until they know how much you care.

2. Be a good example. You cannot expect your people to be what you are not. The leadership is reflected in the team, and the team is reflected in the leadership. That's all there is to it. If people see you working your ass off, busting your butt, treating people fairly, they are more apt to do the same thing.

3. Build an atmosphere and environment in which your team members enjoy working. The only thing you have to work with is other people, so make that environment enjoyable, even though you're going to work them hard. Keep the motto in the back of your mind that you make your team members better on the field by making them happy off the field.

   And that's why I always share the experiences with my players and their wives and kids outside the business room, that's off the football field and in my house, over a glass of wine, or after a charity function or at the opening of their store, or at the birth of their child or at their wedding. The quality of your organization's attitude will be directly proportional to the quality of the atmosphere you as a leader create for them.

4. Next, you define, you delegate, and then you lead. All team members have to know where they fit in and what's expected of them. Then, you have to delegate or give them the responsibility. Even if you don't always agree, this is good for diversity, personal styles recognition, and clear communication. Delegate and let your team or coaches do what they do best

5. The fifth principle I talk about is energy, bringing positive energy to work with you. In addition, be with the attitude that you can out-work your opponent. If your team can't out-work them, at least you can close the gap between where you are now and where you have to be.

111

I always use my third year as an example. I believe we were 38 and 15 my third year in the NFL. 73 percent win—that's hard to do; 9 and 7, 16 and 3, and 13 and 3 in three different pro-organizations and they were all losing.

Work hard and surround yourself with people who will also work hard. If you have to show your team members how to work hard, then do so. When it's all said and done, they respect you.

I got a phone call the other day from Jerry Sizemore. He played right tackle for me at the Eagles for seven years. He was a Pro Bowler three years. He was a first round pick before I ever got there and a fine player. What he talked about was how tough the training camps were, how it made him a better man. He wasn't used to working like that. When I got there, they thought I was crazy. Then, all of a sudden, he felt himself getting better, his Pro-Bowl performances starting to take place, and then, he played in the Super Bowl. I coached him thirty years ago, but he talked about our team's work ethic. So, I say this to our coaches, 'you are either transmitting energy to your people, or you're sapping it from them—one or the other.'

6. Principle number six is build relationships as you implement your team-building process, and this is the part I miss the most. You're in that

process all of the time as a leader. I miss Kendall Gammon. I miss all those guys because I cared. I served, and I found out that the other guy cares too. That's a great feeling when you've been working together, and you find your assistant coaches cared about you and your players cared about you too. It's a great reward, and that's what I miss now.

7. Being real—I call it being authentic. This principle relies on being evaluated as being sincere. You are who you are, whether it's twenty minutes after you won or twenty minutes after you lost. You are what you are as a person, and when you're authentic as a leader, and people see you as authentic, they will handle most of the situations as well as you do. Some of them will handle it better. As a leader, you get payback. Establishing credibility takes a long time, and if you haven't earned it, you can't use it. If you've earned it, it lasts forever.

"So, make sure they know you care, be a great example, build an atmosphere that they enjoy working, define, delegate, and lead. Work, bring energy, work your butt off, and they will too. Build a relationship as you work through your process and be evaluated as being sincere. You do those things, and you have a leadership process that's going to be very effective."

LEADER'S POINT OF VIEW

For Dick Vermeil, one person's leadership style starts with how you look at things, your vision.

Vermeil:

"I thought my responsibility, as a leader, was to always sell the vision of being the best you could be in our trade. My role was to help the individual define their role or position within that vision.

"Next was the vision of the best we can be as a football team, like the time we hoisted the Lombardi Trophy high so all could see it. You delegate and you establish a process. How you're going to go about it, your organizational scheme like practice routines, meeting routines, and travels. Within the vision and routine, you are building relationships. I don't coach football. I coach people who play football for a living."

Remember:

- ☑ Everybody is critically important on the team.

- ☑ Yet, there are no superstars on this team.

- ☑ Everybody is going to fall into the team-building process and work to help us be a winning team.

Tony Richardson, my colleague in the Chiefs and now fullback for the New York Jets, also offers his perspective on team building through respect.

Richardson:

"I think the most effective leaders in team building welcome team members of equal ability and confidence. A head coach would say, 'I'm going to empower all of my coaches, my players, and the people around me.' When you do that, the more leaders you can empower. You can delegate effectively. You trust your team to complete their tasks.

"You have to be secure in yourself. You have to know who you are as a leader in order to empower team members. You've seen guys who aren't very secure in themselves or in their abilities. They want to micromanage everything.

"The most effective head coaches in the National Football League are those who see all their assistant coaches as head coaches. They say, 'I'm not going to tie them down. I'm not going to strap them down to where they can't talk to the media, where they can't do anything like that.' In turn you can transfer and delegate from the assistant head coach down to your players in leadership. The players can take over; take care of their running back group or their wide receiver group or their special teams group. Now that's a team because everyone's really speaking the same language."

KENDALL GAMMON

CONCLUSION

The leaders who contributed to this book described that the leader creates the team environment, which supports open communication, brainstorming, and acceptance of all team members. In addition, the team comes together around the leader's vision or manager's goal for the team. Commitment to the organizational purpose provides a clear sense of direction and becomes members' motivation to accomplish their assignments. An effective team's power is proportionate to the skills members possess and their efforts and energy that members expend.

CHAPTER SEVEN

Advice for Rookies from the Locker Room

Leadership is a matter of having people look at you
and gain confidence, seeing how you react.
If you're in control, they're in control.

Tom Landry

INTRODUCTION

The National Football League hosts the highest
profile sport in America, and, I feel, one of the most
violent. There is constant pressure on the coaches
and players to perform. Winning is expected and
losing is never tolerated, at least not for long. Most
NFL players were leaders at the college level, and
their skills elevated their status so that coaches
and scouts noticed. Some players led vocally while

others were quieter, letting their actions speak for them. Someone who rises to notice will naturally develop an ego.

A REALISTIC EGO

A person with a healthy ego recognizes their value, skills, and their worth to the game. They have a good sense of self worth. In this context, ego means an appropriate level of importance or value to the team and the game.

A player with an unhealthy ego demonstrates an exaggerated sense of their importance. Other people might view this kind of player as arrogant or as a braggart. Players with healthy egos become healthy leaders because they are in control of their emotions and manage their life with vision. Persons with unhealthy egos have few trusted friends, feel insecure, and are not in control of life events. Generally, they are not team players.

An NFL team, then, is filled with highly skilled leaders with highly evolved egos. In this day and age, healthy egos and leadership walk hand-in-hand. Not only is this necessary, it is also healthy.

In the Kansas City Chiefs' weight room, a sign on the wall reads, "Check your Ego at the door." Over the years, people perceive the word "ego" in a broad spectrum of meanings, including self-confidence, self-assurance, and assertiveness. These attributes are needed for an individual's as well as the team's success.

- If you believe in yourself, you radiate confidence.

- Then others feel confident with you and depend upon you.

On the other hand, the negative interpretation of "ego" implies being distracted by your own importance. This can come from a person's basic sense of insecurity in working with others, or it can spring from a person's need to draw attention to himself. Ego, defined in the above manner, makes the outcome of team success difficult.

Remember, all people have egos. It's up to the coach or leader to harness the talents and direct the energy of team members. Realize also that egos are not only present, but also necessary.

As the one in charge, it's up to you to shape the egos in pursuit of the ultimate goal, be it the Super Bowl in the NFL, or success in the business world. Do this, and you will lead leaders.

EGOS, BELIEFS, AND ROLES

Ego is an important part of self-image. In the world of leadership, ego may be confused with personal beliefs as well as the role you happen to be playing. For example, in a family, a parent can easily confuse their role of parent with the beliefs they have about that role. Listen to this conversation between a dad and his eleven-year-old son.

"You almost knocked that ball for a homer, son."

"Yeah, Dad. I'm just not good enough."

"Don't think that way, son. You've got to be more positive."

"I'm trying. I'm trying. I'm just disappointed right now that I didn't make a homer."

"Well, why don't we practice more at home?"

"Dad, I already practice every day after school."

In reality, all Dad had to do was listen. He has a healthy parenting ego and has a good relationship with his son. However the role of "Dad" in this family focuses on sports, so Dad believes it is his task to help his son along and offers shallow suggestions not relevant to the missed homer. It is okay for his son to feel bad, and Dad doesn't need to fix it simply because he believes that's what a dad should do.

In a business meeting, confusion between healthy ego and beliefs about a role could unfold like this scenario: "Lisa" was conducting a brainstorming session, whose rules allowed all ideas to be voiced, listed, and discussed. Some heated debate ensued as to the best course of action for this group to determine and follow. Lisa believed in being "nice." Being nice included letting people argue during this brainstorming, not defining boundaries, and moving the group beyond brainstorming to resolution. She confused leading with a belief that leaders are nice. Lisa could easily have defined boundaries, completed the brainstorming session, and moved to a new arena of making a group decision in a nice way. A nice leader doesn't mean being permissive, as Lisa believed. Her vision of herself as a leader didn't leave room for healthy ego in the areas of debate, challenges, or criticism.

Lisa did not demonstrate a healthy ego in this meeting.

Not having enough ego affects our ability to lead and make a difference as well. Lisa wanted to be liked and accepted as the group leader. Not having enough ego to be confident within your role can also appear as:

- Being embarrassed when someone disagrees with you or asks you a challenging question

- Compromising too easily

- Avoiding the truth of the situation or beating around the bush

- Feeling intimidated when you think others are more powerful or higher in rank

- Feeling afraid to make a mistake

- Swallowing your words or not speaking up when you feel the urge

Next, contrast the behavior of an unhealthy ego with the actions that are congruent to a healthy ego.

- Sharing any idea you believe to have value
- Not taking disagreement personally, understanding everyone will believe as they wish, and you may or may not influence them
- Including boundary definitions, laying ground rules, and providing criticism
- Risking hurt feelings; you may find others respect you instead
- Disagreeing with your ideas does not mean you are being rejected
- Savoring mistakes and relishing what you can learn

In the book, *egonomics: What Makes Ego Our Greatest Asset (or Most Expensive Liability)* (Fireside, 2007), authors Steve Smith and David Marcum indicate that successful leaders start with a healthy ego and big ideas, ambition, and a vision for their success. People talk around egos and discuss topics like how to communicate and make better financial decisions.

So let's agree for the purpose of this book that a healthy ego, as opposed to a high-and-mighty ego, is a necessary component in self worth. A healthy ego demonstrates personal belief in your ability to carry through and being willing to walk your talk with passion.

The authors of *egonomics* also make the point that everyone experiences a bit of an inflated ego sometimes, especially if we have been through tough times and have felt powerless or helpless. Ego, at those times, is like an inflated balloon—we hope an inflated ego will lift us out of feeling powerless if we can hang on. The authors pointed out four early warning signs, accompanied by negative thoughts, of an inflated ego.

Defending – *I'm right. They're wrong.* Mine is better. In a defensive stance, the corrective posture is to take a step back and get a view of the bigger picture. Instead of stating opinions, ask questions.

Comparing – *I can do it faster, better, etc. Criticize them, go ahead. Mine is better. Mine is worse.* In a mindset of constantly comparing, the corrective behavior is to bring your viewpoint back home. Focus on what you do, how you do it, and use all of your nervous energy to move yourself and your ideas or products ahead.

Desiring recognition or acceptance – *See me! I can do it better. Hey you, appreciate me! Look at me! Aren't I good?* Sometimes, the child within each of us likes appreciation. When you don't get it, a person with a healthy ego knows how to appreciate himself, or allow another the praise they deserve with graciousness.

Showcasing brilliance – *I am the best! My ideas win. Everybody is watching me and cheering me on.* People who need to showcase their brilliance often do so at another's expense. A high ego is not the same as a healthy ego. Everyone respects brilliance, which is partnered with humility, integrity, and credibility.

The authors of *egonomics* remind us that a healthy ego is confident, and doesn't have to prove itself. Healthy ego has an objective mind, values, and passion, and respect for others.

> Good leaders keep their minds open. But great leaders open the minds of others in the most intense circumstances, even against the odds of prejudice, politics, and habit.[iii]
>
> **David Marcum and Steven Smith** *(egonomics)*

HOW DO YOU GET IN YOUR WAY?

Focus versus Distraction

Winning requires focus. In fact, a major secret to winning in any game and achieving success is focus. You can control whatever you focus on, that includes long snapping, parenting, being aware, and remaining positive. Focus takes the place of excuses like, "I can't," and "I'll try."

Andersen:

"Being distracted makes people less effective. They get derailed, you know, they forget what got them there. Dick Vermeil said that we don't win the locker, you know. We rent it. We can't forget that or get distracted by it."

Entitlement versus Humility

Entitlement means that a player in the game seeks credit without having earned it—a sign of an unhealthy ego. Seasoned leaders and players have more humility because of having paid their dues, understanding the bigger vision of their team, and their contribution to it. A humble person knows their answer to the big question of why they are doing what they do.

Andersen:

"Yes I think one of the biggest problems in business, in sports, in society, is that too many people have a false sense of entitlement. Having not earned it is a huge problem. That problem has no business in sports and high level pro-sports. You have to earn the right to be on your team.

"A sense of entitlement is like arrogance. There's a fine line between confidence and arrogance. We have to have confidence, but step over the line into arrogance, and that derails things as well, doesn't it?

"Arrogance is false confidence, exaggerating your skills or your influence. Some people are very successful and arrogant, but it bleeds confidence from the rest of the team. It's not necessarily always a bad thing and depends on how you present it."

Lack of Preparation

Like focus, preparation is an absolute necessity. Trent Green describes how amazed he was as he watched an inspiring leader prepare for a game.

Green:

"Several coaches early on had an impact on me through their sharing what they thought being a leader was. I just watched their preparation, how they approached practice, and their enthusiasm. The person that probably initially jumped out for me would be Coach Mallory, my head coach in Indiana. I already had a good work ethic when I got to Indiana. He showed me that hard work doesn't necessarily guarantee success, but at least you're giving yourself a shot. He worked hard himself and never complained. Just when you thought he was there to give you a pat on the back, he could be more demanding. He helped me take my level of preparations, in fact, my whole game to a whole new level.

"He didn't complain. I remember I found out a couple of days after we had played a game, on Friday afternoon after practice, he was a big, avid horse rider, and he had fallen off his horse and broken a couple of ribs. The pride factor for him is he didn't want any of his players to know because we were getting ready for a game on Saturday. You see, he didn't want to interrupt the preparation. So he went through the whole game doing his screaming and yelling routines. He never told a trainer, a doctor, or anybody until after the game. Then they had the trainers come into the coaches' locker room and look at it. That behavior defined his leadership. He wasn't going to mess with the preparation of the team getting ready for Saturday.

"For my mental preparation, that would have been in my second year in the league with Washington. Coaches Norv Turner and Cam Cameron taught me to take my mental preparation to the next level. You know, I went to San Diego my rookie year, and my whole thing was just out-work everybody. I made sure I was number one in attendance. I made sure I was early to everything. So when I got cut the second year, I said, 'Listen, I've done everything you've asked me to do. I'm number one on all your charts here.' And they're like, 'Yeah, but there's some other things we need you to you improve on.'

"That was really eye-opening for me because I always thought I'd out-work everybody, and they can't get rid of me. When they cut me, and then I got back in the league with Washington and Norv and Cam, I understood the physical preparation. I understood what the commitment was from a physical part and out-working everybody. But the mental part is what changed for me in Washington with Norv and Cam because they wanted me to approach the game like a coach. They wanted me to have the game plan studied and my preparation down cold; to know what everybody's doing; know the shifts and movements of all the receivers, know the formations like the back of your hand; know the protection so well that you can tell

129

Vermeil's Advice to Rookies

People retain fifty percent of what they learn after ten minutes, and only twenty-five percent after forty-eight hours. Whether you are a member of a team preparing for a game, or creating your game plan, follow these steps to efficient learning.

☑ Always be present with others and hear, pay attention to what they say.

☑ Take detailed notes.

☑ Review all information, and if you don't understand, ask questions, and then ask more questions.

☑ Time is a scarce commodity that you manage by choice. Take and make time to invest in your game plan, go way beyond anything you've ever done.

☑ Concentrate and focus on every goal in your game plan. Visualize what you expect consistently.

☑ Knowledge only belongs to you once you have obtained it. Once you have it, use it!

☑ Don't ever wind down mentally. Losing your mental edge means mistakes. Focus mean success.

☑ The concentration and focus in preparing for success has to be excellent always, regardless of circumstances.

☑ Today, any day, your challenge is to adapt, accelerate, innovate, learn, and transform.

☑ Enjoy your success. You deserve it.

the offensive linemen what they're doing, who they're turning to, their responsibilities; the backs' responsibility. That mental preparation carries over into routes and the running game and all those things. So that's really where things changed mentally for me was my first year in Washington in '95."

Andersen:

"I think that preparation is important. One snap doesn't make it good or bad for you and shouldn't define your ability as a snapper. I think you know if you have a bad pre-game, and we've all had them. Preparation is a warm up. You're warming up to perform, so the most important thing that you're trying to accomplish in the pre-game preparation is to warm up, to stroke the ball, and to feel comfortable with your physicality kicking the football. Yet, you know, your mental work should have been done a long time ago. If you're not mentally clear and focused and ready to roll Sunday afternoon, you know it's certainly not going to happen."

Andersen has an excellent point in that the mental and physical strength and preparation deserve equal consideration and focus. When I practice snapping a ball, my mind envisions the game-day with cheering crowds and pressures, so I am snapping in a game, not just in practice. In a player's mind, they are one and the same. The result is your focus and effect, not the conditions around you.

Morten and I used to talk often about our pre-game warm-ups. As a snapper, it is hard to be "perfect" as the arbitrary. The spiral could always be tighter, or the snap itself could always be quicker. Early on, I came to realize the truer meaning of perfection, which is consistency and persistence of practice.

For a kicker, however, it is much more cut and dry. You either make it or you miss it. I've always observed how my kicker was doing in warm-ups. Was he striking the ball well? Was the ball flight normal? Was he following through? Was he making his kicks? My relationship as a snapper to the kicker is akin to the pitcher-catcher relationship in baseball. I was monitoring all aspects I could and giving feedback when necessary. If you're wondering how I can critique a kicker, as a snapper, take into account that I probably snapped a ball for the kicker and watched the process some 30,000 times during my career. Then also realize that I watched film of those same 30,000 kicks, often more than once. Sometimes, when things weren't going as well as the kicker wanted, I sensed it was my time to "step in" and offer the good points of what he was doing. I would remind him of the fact that we've been doing this for years, it's not completely about success right now in warm-ups, rather getting ready physically for the success I "knew" they were going to have in the game.

CONCLUSION

The two words, which summarize the most consistent advice the rookies receive from the locker room, are focus and persistence. Without these key traits, being able to serve on any team and grow in leadership skills is questionable.

Remember that a team member with a healthy ego demonstrates confidence and ability in their skill. They also are consistent in their contributions to the game. Because there is no sense of entitlement in a healthy ego, you'll usually find a colleague who is also humble and helpful to others.

CHAPTER EIGHT

Being Your Own Self-Coach

Be careful what you pretend to be because you are
what you pretend to be.

Kurt Vonnegut

All rookies know the intensity of having a scout
check out their skills, paying attention to their
speed, dexterity, and strength. They play their best,
no pretending. They are as authentic and genuine
as they will ever be when a scout is watching their
performance, for the scout represents the coach
and the team. Later the rookie is consistently
evaluated by a coach and given the game plan
for skill development, all in keeping with making
him a better player and team member. When
the rookie matures to become a leader, he is
still evaluated by colleagues. How can you stay
authentic and on top of your game while being

constantly observed and evaluated?

Two basic skills enable a leader to achieve this goal: self-awareness and self-coaching.

Self-awareness means knowing yourself. Style(s), values, work habits, emotional patterns, motivators, and talents. You may have noticed that the strategies in this book are designed to help you be aware of yourself.

Self-coaching is the ability to coach yourself through skills and drills, or shape your personal interaction with people and tasks. It is through self-coaching steps that you establish your game plan, take action, and be accountable.

The leaders in this book have discussed their work ethic and success habits. They demonstrate that you have to be your own coach, keep up your skills yourself, check your attitude every morning and several times throughout the day to manage a successful game plan. Do you measure your personal effectiveness? Do you challenge yourself? Can you draw an analogy between how you look at your habits and your ability to lead successfully? Let's discuss self-awareness and self-coaching in more detail.

SELF-AWARENESS

People with self-awareness are successful in their game plan and become leaders because they have strong intuition and the ability to read other people and respond appropriately to them. Self-awareness means you know your moods, preferences and resources. Being aware means that you also notice the world around you. You are attentive to what goes on, and you are also responsive if you need to be. A perfect example is the aware parent who can decipher a young child's antics or misbehavior as a need to be fulfilled rather than a willful attack on the parent. Another example is a manager who observes that a worker's low performance may be due to an illness, and can discuss the matter with compassion and directness.

Not all people are comfortable with self-reflection. Yet self-reflection correlates highly with confidence and achievement. Having little self-awareness implies that a leader may not be aware of his weaknesses and, as a result, may be unable to manage emotional states. One may lack the confidence that comes from challenging himself and achieving his goals.

Self-awareness is built upon honesty and feedback, from yourself or others. Here's Andersen's take on the topic.

Andersen:

"I think self-awareness so important in improving as a player or as a leader. I do performance feedback sheets after each game; I evaluate every practice kick. I videotape every practice kick, every game kick. So I think criteria, specific criteria, enable you to give yourself objective feedback, and I'm always tougher on myself than anybody else would be.

"If you want to get to a higher level, perhaps to the highest level, then you look at your performance and find the room for improvement. What are your criteria for challenging yourself? Identify the problems, and then identify the patterns in the problems. Why are you doing that? Can you identify what the underlying problem is? We're not looking for symptoms, we're looking for what's the reason, and I think that's where self-scouting and performance feedback really can help you. I use video analysis, and I film everything because I don't want to leave anything to chance.

"Let's say you're struggling. You've missed a couple of kicks and your confidence went south, or you feel like you've been punched in the stomach. Well, how do you get back to basics? You go back and look at your successes, and then you just build it up from the basics again. That's how you're able to continue, and to continue to improve. Don't be scared. Don't be scared of distasteful situations. Everybody's going to have those, and it's how you deal with them."

I like Andersen's points about the fact that all of us have failures and make mistakes, and when we do, we start again on the task and move it to the next level. What I take from that is, "don't settle for where you are" and don't just do the minimum. Anticipate your problems and head them off at the pass by finding solutions ahead of time. That is what self-awareness can do for you!

Think of the business leader who implemented a nominal plan that worked for him. His marketing director launched his product, ran an effective advertising campaign, and had moderate success. The business owner would have liked it to turn out better, but he lets it go. I say, don't stop there. Be the self-coach. Do a critical analysis on your performance, always looking at the detail. This self-awareness empowers you to take control of such situations and makes a substantial difference in your success rate. Being tough on yourself is okay, and so is being realistic. Be the self-coach. Go back to your game plan and reanalyze.

SELF-COACHING

Self-coaching is your ability to motivate yourself to take action. You are aware, can make appropriate choices, and change the course of what isn't working. Self-coaching means changing habits that hinder realizing your goals and achieving your game plan. Behavioral change is not always easy, but a strong leader tackles inner resistance and brings the victory home. In my first book, *Life's a Snap!*, I discussed proven self-coaching strategies to identify and change patterns of thoughts and feelings that limit you, distract you, or keep you from achieving your goals.

Positive Self-Talk: Negative self-talk is a wonderful downer, and toxic to your mental health. If your thoughts are filled with what you cannot do and the impossible dreams you will never fulfill, then snap out of it. Refocus your awareness to positive self-talk. This works wonders when a child is frightened or an adult believes that their next business steps are too challenging. Feel these words as you think them: *I am willing to move forward. I take the first step. I know how to succeed and I am doing so now. I can do this. I am doing this. I can see and feel my success. I am successful.* Get the idea? Snap to it!

Positivity: In high-pressure situations, as in business or in a game, there is simply no room for negative thinking or downward-spiraling emotions. Your positive attitude and energy have to be *high* to carry you and your team members through game pressures, tense plays, and encounters. Skilled leaders do this, and the task requires diligence in your awareness.

Self-challenges: Accountability is built into your game plan to successful leadership. Perhaps you are accountable to team members, a partner, or manager. Ultimately you are responsible to yourself and for yourself, and the following steps are what I use to challenge myself to do better.

- Maximize your performance all the time. Raise the bar until you make it, and then raise the bar again.

- Make it as perfect as you can. Perfection is your aim, your goal, and practice will keep you shooting for that goal.

- Realize you're a human being and not a perfect machine.
- Have fun striving and thriving. Your smile lets others know that life is good!

Self-coaching was a central leadership trait for Trent Green, as he explains it. He challenged himself in the minute ways when observing how he and his teammates played.

Green:

"Self-coaching was always an important part for me. We'd go through a scouting meeting to review another team's tendencies; we were looking for something to give us an advantage. Whether it was a linebacker whose stance changed when he was rushing or dropping or the certain way a particular defensive end moved around corners.

"I was always very attuned to watch my moves on a tape to make sure, whether it be my hands, my feet, my head, my shoulders, if there was something I was giving away, not only in the huddle, but at the line of scrimmage with the cadence. Did I stare down the receiver that time? Yeah I did, but the time before, I looked him off."

Green describes how one team scouts other players on other teams. We watch and learn from each other. And we observe our errors, we automatically self-correct those mistakes. For example, Trent would observe the rhythm of cadence, certain voice inflections, certain colors, and numbers that he was using. The ability to be aware and discipline himself according to what the game calls for is further explained.

Green:

> "You know I was very conscious of what I incorporated into the plan. If we have a lot of 'check with me' this week that we're using certain colors and numbers, I would make sure we would use those colors and numbers within the course of the cadence. You never know. I mean there are a lot of guys that don't pay any attention to that, but you never know when one linebacker might pay attention. All of sudden, he gets a jump on me. So I was always very conscious of all those things."

WAYS TO SHIFT FROM SELF-CENTERED TO SERVICE

I have observed that when rookies are learning to be leaders, they may confuse self-centeredness with being aware of self and others. Self-centeredness is about that unhealthy ego we discussed in earlier chapters. The unhealthy ego is based on self-interest and entitlement, comes across as arrogant, and reeks of fear that a dog could smell a mile away. The following self-coaching strategies enable one to turn self-centeredness into healthy leadership skills, if he is willing and committed to become a service-oriented leader.

Shift Entitlement to Service
Richardson:

"Coach Vermeil used to say, 'Don't ask people around you to do something that you're not willing to do yourself.' I think if you can show others that you know you aren't too big to run out there and get tea or make some copies if you're in an office, then you demonstrate the willingness to help, be of service, and lend a hand. Once the people around you see that, it really turns on a light for them if it takes everyone to do what we're trying to do. If it's coaching professional football, high school football, or elementary football, everyone's in it together. Would you trust a boss in the boardroom who threw away his own coffee cup, or the one who left it to you to clean up?

"Through one person's willingness or service, there is a domino effect. It doesn't matter who gets the credit. We're all on the same page and we're all out here working for the same goal."

> It's amazing what can be accomplished when no one cares who gets the credit.
>
> **Coach Dick Vermeil**

Shift Arrogance to Accountability
Richardson:

"I think things are earned and nothing is deserved. To feel that you deserve without earning is arrogance. I think that's the message that you have to send. If you work hard and bust your butt, you achieve a goal. That you've earned it is more meaningful, but there's nothing if you ever walk around in a situation and feel like, oh I'm in a position of entitlement and I deserves this or I deserve that. I think respect is earned, trust is earned, and when people can sense that, then they know. He's a guy just like me and we're all in this thing together. I think it really motivates your people under you and motivates the people around you to go out and give it their all. Then you're accountable to each other."

Shift Fearfulness to Fearlessness

Fearless is not the absence of fear. In her book, *On Becoming Fearless ... In Love, Work and Life* (Little Brown and Company, 2006), author Arianna Huffington calls fearlessness the mastery of fear. I think of fear as our primal feeling of vigilance that kept us safe in other times in history. So we want fear to be our friend, and then we ride the adrenaline we feel to achieve our desires.

Once, a friend shared with me that her daughter was "scared to go to that new school." Rather than give advice, the mother asked, "How would you like to handle that "scare." The eight-year-old said, "Lets just call scary, excited." So they changed their language to the excitement the daughter felt to go to a new school. The young girl's self-coaching taught us a great lesson for leadership.

A friend of mine who is a public speaker openly discusses his dread and fear of getting on stage. Once he is on stage, he is a superb entertainer. For him, it is walking on stage, under bright lights, and facing his audience. He uses a positive mental attitude to pace before going on stage, works his energy to a high level, and jumps on stage with a big hello. Once he makes eye contact with his audience, he transforms into an inspirational man.

I have always thought fear was really my greatest ally in my career. The uncertainty of how long my career would last drove me to challenge myself, raise the bar, and develop my skills and expertise to the next level. The fear of losing my job actually helped me maintain a marvelous fifteen career in the NFL, where the average career for players is three years. The strength of fearlessness can carry a leader a long way in rising to the challenges of leadership.

Build Credibility Through Caring

Coach Vermeil was big on the theme of caring for his assistant coaches and players. "People don't care how much you know until they know how much you care," was his favorite adage. In addition to Vermeil, Bobby April always made this point.

Once April and I had a talk in New Orleans. He asked me to reflect on what he did better than others and things he didn't do as well. I was always impressed with April's ability to know the guy's first and last names. He always made a conscious effort to know how to pronounce them. People love hearing their name, but hate hearing it pronounced wrong. He knew what colleges the guys came from. He made a very conscious effort to develop relationships, and those small efforts go a long way towards getting people to perform on special teams. I asked him to address building credibility through caring.

April:

"For me that's what I try to focus on in my small, very small role as a leader of a certain segment of a team. So while you're leading the person, you're treating them like you would treat anybody else, which raises your credibility.

"They know you care because you care about the dignity of that person and let's face it, I mean, one of the greatest possessions a person has is his name. By knowing his background, you're telling him that you care about his life. When you talk about the fact he's from this high school or this college, you tell him that you care about his life and that you had enough consideration of him that you would find about who he is, what he is, and what he's not. Wow, I mean how can you lead that guy if he sees himself as a piece of merchandise? You're not going to be a very good leader if you cannot build your team through caring. You're only strong as your weakest link."

The country is full of good coaches. What it takes to win is a bunch of interested players.

Don Coryell, ex-San Diego Chargers coach

April:

"I had a player this week that we had to make a change on something. I called him in and told him why we were going to do this. He was disappointed, but he was grateful that somebody communicated with him. He echoed to me that generally he doesn't get that kind of consideration; that is crazy. I mean here's a guy that's playing in the National Football League. In his hometown he's one of the biggest things that ever happened, and he's at a place where he feels like nobody gives him consideration? It is kind of mind boggling. In a high-pressured game, tense business situations, or in everyday interactions, caring does build your credibility."

I totally support Coach April's view. In any position in life, leadership is about building rapport and respect with your team. I always took pride in the fact that I was an NFL Player's Association rep as elected by my teammates. I will always believe that they elected me to this position because I cared about what happened to them during their career, and moreover, took a personal interest in their personal lives. I made time to explain anything and everything they asked, be it career-related or how to find a preschool for their child. In essence, they knew that I while I wasn't required to take the time to help them, I chose to do so because of my values as a service-oriented leader.

CONCLUSION

All of us stay on the top of our most authentic game when we are able to observe our actions and hold ourselves accountable for our results. Self-coaching for leadership is like having a conversation with yourself, day in and day out, about being comfortable in your roles and personal responsibilities. Self-coaching empowers you to keep discovering how you can help others, which skills you want to sharpen, or how can you make a difference today.

Success lies in being your genuine self, willing to make choices that move you into your success stream. Only you can know how to realize your leadership vision, and, by connecting with your team, create a foundation and game plan for success.

CHAPTER NINE

Lessons For Winning

Adversity causes some men to break;
others to break records.

William A. Ward

I originally titled this chapter *Lessons from Losing* because losing is a reality in life with which we all deal. As a parent who attends my sons' sporting events, and as a player on the NFL field, I take notice of the sore losers, the angry losers, or the hurt losers, and I observe that they have the same responses in any aspect of the game. We don't need to learn how to lose gracefully; we need to learn how to be gracious people whether we win or lose. So the title chapter morphed into the reality of our game plans for life; that is, lessons for winning.

In my research for this book, there wasn't much out there on the psychology of losing, and a wide array on the psychology of winning. This reflects our social and cultural attitudes about the game plan. Play to win! And why not? Winning is a thrill, a rush!

What I have learned over the years about playing "the game" in our society is that by focusing on winning, we create our character who plays the game with the right attitude and actions, learning the leadership skills discussed in this book. So what attitudes work best for winning?

- Enter the game to win!
- Set goals to achieve them! Be proactive in this.
- Take the necessary affirmative action for the game plan.
- Never look back, and keep moving ahead.

While winning is the goal of the game plan, these attitudes may work well until adversity challenges our characters. Only then, as leaders, do we measure the strength of our coping skills or resilience. In other words, how do we handle losing or facing situations in which we've lost control?

The greatest test of courage on earth is to bear defeat without losing heart.

Robert Ingersoll

WINNING AND LOSING

Richardson:

"Early in my football career I had a tough time with losing. I was in Kansas City, and we'd lose a game and I'd be in the dumps. I'd have my family in town and I wouldn't want to go to dinner. I'd just want to go in the room and just kind of put my head under the pillow. That could be one game. It could have been the first game of the season, in the middle of the season, or a playoff game. I didn't really handle that too well.

"As I started to get older, now I never want to ever get dissatisfied with losing. If I do have a bump in the road, a setback in life, lose a ball game, drop a pass, or miss a block, I use them now as learning experiences. I try to stay on an even keel through the highs and lows. I used to beat myself tremendously, and so my big thing now is go out and play as well as I prepare myself to play; go out and do my job to the best of my ability. Today, I just put my best foot forward. I can continue to keep working hard and try to change the results the next time. I think with that attitude you can be successful in life."

In their book called *Winning* (HarperCollins, 2005), Jack and Suzie Welch boil all of the questions on parenting, business, life, and corporate America to one question: *What does it take to win?* They state that winning has to happen cleanly and by the rules of the game.

In their philosophy, talent matters, but *character*

matters more. Remember Vince Lombardi's pronouncement that "winning isn't everything; it's the only thing." That was the basis of game plans of yesteryear, not in contemporary times. Emphasis on winning cheats us of the character lessons that need to be learned on the way to winning the game, the character lessons of losing that make a real winner. The contributing leaders to this book, my associates of the previous decades, have emphasized the characteristics of caring, service, and helping team members reach their peak to maximize their performance. This builds inner motivation and a sense of accomplishment. Moreover, it enables the character of a person to withstand the losses and sustain their vision when losing. So what is character, really?

CHARACTER

Have you read a great book because you identified with a character? You liked the qualities of their personality, perhaps even shared similar values to that. Your family members, team players and business colleagues identify with you as a leader because of the nature and quality of your character, which refers to your mental and moral strengths.

The main character lesson for winning is doing your best or giving it your all. From the time we are children, however, we don't know what our best is until we stretch our minds and push our physical limits. Wow, then we discover that we have some talent and abilities, which lead us to develop achievement patterns. Then we start practicing or training those skills.

Practice works for the brain and body by establishing what we call memory traces or neural patterns. If you ride a bike long enough, it feels like a habit that you can recall when you need to. More practice strengthens those patterns that you call on when you want to perform. Knowing this gives you the mental edge in the game. You learn to trust yourself and display confidence in your skills. Then, you know you've done your best.

The focus and intensity you bring to practice trains your brain and body to win. In fact, the more pressure the better; as you stretch to perform, your body remembers. Momentum is also important— once you are there, keep going.

An interesting perception starts to form for children when they find enjoyment and pleasure in their tasks. Activities that they engage in "for the love of the game" become their successful endeavors. That is, their momentum and motivation to want to practice, enjoy their skill building, and learn to challenge themselves to do better.

CHALLENGE OF LOSING

Sports psychologist, John F. Murray, Ph.D., gives straight talk about losing in his article, "Losing with Style."[iv] Whether a player is a perfectionist or

155

emotionally immature, there are four ways to handle defeat. Murray suggests:

1. **Immediate congratulations** to the winner. When you walk up to the winner with a handshake, a pat on the back, and heart-felt congratulations, the sting of losing isn't nearly as disheartening.

2. **Learning from the incident** is the most valuable character trait one could gain from losing. I call it *analyze and realize.*

3. **Never making excuses** is one way to quiet that inner voice, which tends to ask *Why me? Why now? How did I lose?* The berating voice continues until you stop it. The way to deal with that inner gremlin is to snap out of it. Then analyze and realize. *Analyze your mistakes; realize your lessons.*

4. **Displaying humor** helps you manage the adrenalin comedown after a pumped-up game effort.

These four steps are good advice, and very similar to the message we hear in the NFL, as Vrabel suggests.

Vrabel:

"I think you learn more about losing than you do winning. You learn what you need to work on. You learn what you need to improve. You need to learn how to win close games by knowing what you did wrong or where you made the mistake. Everybody can know how to play a certain situation. Yet, it's being able to go out there under pressure, perform, and making the right play."

Analyzing and realizing, then, may mean the difference in our character's success when facing adversity or losing. Apply what we've learned and practice those skills for improvement. Who doesn't need to improve their game plan?

In the heat of competition, there's pressure. In the heat of pressure, there's your focus and your skills. Within you, is the memory of how to win! Do you trust yourself to act in the heat of pressure? Do you have inner toughness to rise up as a resilient warrior and love the competition, the battle, the game itself? So maybe we love the game itself, the money, the glamour, and in the end, we ask the same question of ourselves: How do we respond in the second half of the game?

How you respond to the challenge in the second half will determine what you become after the game, whether you are a winner or a loser.

Lou Holtz

Let me share a little known secret about losing that will uncover your inner strengths. When we are at our worst moment, we have the ability to be the best ever. When we are most vulnerable, we can find the deeper strength of character within us to win.

- Think back to your teen years or early adulthood to a time of crisis or intense stress, perhaps an incident in which you could have lost or did lose significantly.

- Mentally review your responses during and after the crisis.

- What behaviors did you show or what actions did you take during the crisis that you learned from, that made you a better person?

- Review your actions after the loss. What strength did you learn from the incident and how you handled it?

How did you learn to think clearly in crisis? How did you learn to respond to competition? No retreating, no excuses, no raging unless you can take that wave of emotion and redirect it to the necessary game action. You'll find your strength in what you gained during that time of loss.

For me, the time of loss was in 1988 when my mother was diagnosed with lung cancer. Although we were able to say, "I love you" to each other before her death, I deeply regretted at that time that I'd never have the chance to reconcile my feelings toward her. I relate in *Life's a Snap* that my mother was somewhat in competition with me during my teen years, most likely due to her depression, which I did not understand.

After her death, I thought about leaving Pittsburg State and returning to a smaller local college to help out and be near my dad. That is what my heart wanted to do, and most likely, I'd have regretted the move because it meant giving up my NFL dream and destiny. The stinging voice of my head coach, Dennis Franchione, reminded me that I had made a commitment, and he wanted me to keep my word to play for his team, which was my team. I think originally I thought this was a selfish act on his part to keep a good player at the school, and it may have been to some degree. But I learned later that he had lost both of his parents at a young age. I think at some level, he had learned something from his own experiences and felt it best for me to continue in my same environment. Losing my mother was a life-altering event to be sure, however the decision to stay at Pittsburg State University and play football helped shape my destiny in a way I could never have understood at the time.

I learned several strong coping mechanisms from that tough period: to look ahead, move forward and honor my commitments. And those coping skills helped me moved through NFL cuts, my sons' problems at birth, and even through a Super Bowl loss.

YOUR PROFESSIONAL CHARACTER

April:

"It falls totally to your professional character to exert and to go out and give it your all when you're not rewarded. When you are rewarded it all comes a lot easier. Then you've got eleven guys giving their all because they know they're going to be rewarded; like for our field goal block team. I tell them all the time that they've got tremendous professional character and integrity because we have done a good job going after it. We have not blocked, we blocked one in pre-season this year. But that's the only block we've had in four years, and I mean the guys have strained. It's a hell of a statement about who they are and their professional effort and character. I would love to see them rewarded for it, but the fact that they have done that without any reward is tremendous."

MAKING MISTAKES

If you watch a child learning to read, or even better, if you are a parent who reads with your child, you'll have noticed the tiny steps through which a child learns a word. The sound "moo" is associated with the picture of the cow long before the name is learned. The bigger picture is mentally anchored long before the sound and word associations. Then comes the two sounds of "c" and ow" which eventually blend into a semblance of the word cow. Every child will have variations of the "ow" sound, such as "oo" and "o" before a parent's eyes light up and nod a joyful yes at the correct pronunciation. Next that child is motivated to make more sounds and receive those smiling nods of happy parents.

"Live life fully while you're here. Go out and screw up! You're going to anyway, so you might as well enjoy the process. Take the opportunity to learn from your mistakes: find the cause of your problem and eliminate it. Don't try to be perfect; just be an excellent example of being human."

Tony Robbins

Note that the parents never think the child made a mistake and it is bad thing. No! Every effort is a variation of the learning curve, and a step closer to the goal of recognition and naming of cow.

In all of our efforts, there are no mistakes, only variations of steps toward completing the task. A friend of mine, Dr. Caron Goode, tells the story that while completing her doctorate, one professor asked a trick question, "What is the difference in how children and adults learn?" The class members gave near-miss answers with much justification of theory. Goode, recently stepping out of a special education classroom where she had taught *how to learn* to immigrant parents and their children, responded to the professor, "There is no difference."

Few people realize that all human beings, whether children or adults, learn through experience.

We learn through guidance, modeling, and demonstration. We learn by trying, analyzing and realizing, and retrying. There are no mistakes, only steps in learning.

I especially like the riddle used by author, Susan Haldon Brown, in her book, *Mistakes Worth Making: How to Turn Sports Errors into Athletic Excellence* (Human Kinetics Publishers, June 2003): *When is a mistake not a mistake? Anytime you like!*

Brown's point, of course, is that a mistake is in the eye of the beholder. I might see my son's sports efforts as his doing the best he can, while his coach might say the effort is not his best. The mother of a toddler who throws food from the table in glee might see it as a child's mistake and teach him to pick it up, while another mother sees it as a bad behavior and removes the child from the table. I repeat: *There are no mistakes, only steps in learning and variants in performance.*

Here is Kevin Greene's take on the topic of mistakes.

Greene:

> "I think you learn some from a loss and a win. I think there are a lot of wins out there that we had in great games. Like other players in great games, I was very critical of myself cause I could have played better. I mean I had a game where I had a couple of quarterback sacks, maybe a tackle for loss, maybe a couple of batted passes, fumble recovery. I mean there's always room for improvement.

"In my good games, even though I had two or three sacks or whatever, I could have been better. Even in a loss, even if I would have had a good game and a loss, I always ask how could I have played better? Could I have done this better to make a game-changing play to turn the tide? That mindset keeps me alert and aware.

"I mean you can never say you've arrived. You got this big game and you won it. You had a great game, but is that the time to exhale? No. It's time to get the game film out and see what we did right and high-five everybody, swap a little slobber, look what we did wrong and improve."

So when you win or when you're successful in what you're doing, be it business or personal, you still need to analyze and realize. That equates to self-evaluation and self-awareness. Even in being unsuccessful, the loss fits into the overall success theme of a person's life.

Mawae:

"Well, I think you have to evaluate the loss, and obviously take the positives out so you don't beat yourself down mentally that you're totally a loser.

"You've got to look at the positive, but you got to realize, 'we dropped this.' We dropped it, and we have to regroup. Never say die man, I mean, you just have to keep going. Don't let that loss bury you. I think a lot of teams get down a couple three or four games, and maybe they don't have a lot of leaders on their team, but they end up burying themselves just with their mentality. A losing mentality will permeate a team just like a winning mentality will."

"It is never simply a case of win or lose, because I do not demand victory. The significance of the score is secondary to the importance of finding out how good you can be."
John Wooden

CONCLUSION

I have enjoyed Coach Vermeil's teaching methods and talks, which often included fables. One of his favorites was the story of a retiring carpenter who was asked by his employer to stay on to build one more house. While the carpenter agreed, he was tired, and his pride of craftsmanship gone. His worked suffered and showed in the use of inferior materials and careless results. When the employer handed the carpenter the keys to his new home as a surprise retirement gift, the carpenter was shocked and depressed. If only he'd known.

Yes, if only we had all known, what would we do differently? You are the character in your playbook, the carpenter of your life. How you build your future is based upon the attitudes, actions, and choices you make now. Be steadfast in your character so that whether you are winning or losing, you respond with the same strength and compassion in all of your relationships.

Lifetime of Stats
Your Legacy

"The greatest legacy we can leave behind is a memory
of a life lived fully and honorably, a life dedicated to
being the best we can be"

Lou Holz

One self-growth exercise is to write your
obituary and reflect on how you would like to
be remembered. The exercise provides food for
intriguing introspection.

- Would you like to be remembered for
  actions you took?

- Would you desire that others remember
  your stats, what you've achieved?

- How about for the qualities of your relationships?

- Would your contributions be in your philosophy and the thoughts you have shared?

These thought provoking questions remind us that our legacies start now, in this moment, and continue each morning that we awaken and renew our relationships. I believe in leaving a legacy by staying present in the moment in service and awareness.

IN THE MOMENT

April:

> "You're in the moment. I mean 'in the moment' is what's important, not the last play. You're not measuring the past. You're measuring right now and nothing can be more important for a player than the right now."

Who you are today, right here and now is your legacy. Thinking about your game plan from this viewpoint makes you an effective leader and a better person. What you do in this moment defines your impact and influence. Do you think it is important for people to realize that we're impacting each other all the time whether we think so or not? Tony Richardson and I recently had such a discussion.

Richardson:

"Yeah, it's a great question. I was speaking of the NFL experience last night, and someone asked me, 'What is your approach to life? What is your attitude in life?' I told them that as I get older, I realize that the little things like opening the door and holding it for someone or giving someone an encouraging word matter to me. You know, having a smile on your face, having a good, positive attitude. You never know how you might impact another person's life.

"Like with Daryl Johnston, DJ, he didn't realize the impact he was going to have on my life and my career some fifteen years ago. By being himself, which was a person that cared about people and wanted to see people succeed, he didn't have to do it. He was that sort of caring person. You don't really realize the impact that you have in people's lives by giving them encouraging word or pat on the back, or saying you can do this if you work hard. I pray that I have that impact on others."

WALK, WHEN NOT RUNNING THROUGH LIFE

In general, I think people get caught up too much in life and what it is they do, as opposed to who they are to their family. Leaving football, you know, we always say it's the best temporary job we'll ever have. What will you take with you from the NFL that you think will best serve you in the future? Kevin Mawae presents his philosophy on our legacies.

Mawae:

"Well, I tell people all the time that I play football, but I'm a dad, a husband, a friend, a neighbor, an employee. I mean, there's so much more to me, and football happens to be the vehicle by which most people know me. I think what I'll take away from football when I leave is that nothing good comes easy. I think football took me when I was eight years old. I'm thirty-six now, I've been playing for twenty-eight years, and every year is a challenge. Every year, to get up on a Monday morning to go work out at 7:30 with a bunch of twenty-two year olds and keep pace with them is a challenge. Nothing good that you enjoy, that you love, comes easy because if you love it passionately enough, then you make it challenging for yourself. If it's too easy, then it's not worth it.

"I've been blessed. I've been blessed more by good than anything else, and that's where my faith comes in. I mean, as a football player, you live on the edge and you know that this very next play could be your last. There's something in us that we still continue to play the game because God put it in us, though we know that it could be over in an instant.

"I've been given a gift to be able to play a game to make more money than most people will make in a lifetime, and I need to appreciate that. Third, I think that life is not always about you. I think that to get where I am, there were a lot of people involved whether it was a coach, parent, my spouse, my kids. There are a lot people that sacrificed to get to where I am.

"In the NFL, you get so caught up in yourself because

it's a self-driven game, yet you're only a small part of something bigger than yourself. I think I'll always keep that in mind, that there's always something bigger than me. We tell each other that all the time in the locker room, or coaches tell you there's always somebody bigger. There's always going to be somebody faster. There's always going to be somebody stronger or smarter. The one thing that I'll miss, I'm sure you've probably experienced it, is having like-minded people around you. That leader is having a vision that everybody else can buy into, and then keeping everything focused to the big picture. I think those four or five things can keep you in good stead outside of football and any business realm that you're in."

YOUR SPHINX

Of the many architectural wonders of the world, the Sphinx has always amazed me. While I marvel at the construction, I give more thought to its purpose. Was it simply a legacy for the pharaoh of a dynasty? What did the monument mean for the architect who designed it and the stonemason who helped to build it?

Our legacies will result from our relationships and people's memories of us, how we've lived and interacted. Perhaps our hearts will be the monuments people remember. In case you are beginning to think this is an idealistic approach, here is a real life example of one of the most winning coaches of all time, John Wooden, the basketball coaching legend. Wooden coached the ULCA Bruins basketball team for nearly a quarter century, and set records that are still unmatched. He created a dynasty in college basketball. He won ten national NCAA championships in twelve years. His team, from 1972—1974, played two perfect seasons—eighty-eight games without a loss. Never in college basketball history had this been done, and it hasn't been done since. What a legacy!

How did he do it? Although Wooden did not necessarily understand that his actions were "outward-focused," or that his coaching style complied with the Law of Contribution, his approach exemplifies the leadership of service described by the contributors to the book.

In his book *My Personal Best* (McGraw-Hill, 2004), Wooden suggested, "that one of the reasons UCLA often outscored opponents was that I never stressed outscoring opponents—that is, 'beating' someone else or 'needing' to win a game."…"Try your hardest, make the effort, do your best. That's what I stressed…."

He said, "the 'score' that matters most is the one that measures your effort—and ultimately, only you know the score." John Wooden's definition of success was, "Success is peace of mind, which is a direct result of self-satisfaction in knowing you did your best to become the best that you are capable of becoming."

When you contribute to others, when you live your life helping others meet their needs, you get what you want, and your life becomes significant in ways you cannot anticipate. Your legacy is in your living.

[i] "What Is Resiliency?" Global Resiliency Network,
www.globalresiliency.net

[ii] Blair Singer, "The Introduction," The ABC's of Building a
Business Team That Wins: The Invisible Code of Honor That
Takes Ordinary people and Turns Them Into a Championship
Team. (Business Plus, 2004, p. xix)

[iii] David Marcum, Steven Smith, egonomics: What Makes Ego
Our Greatest Asset (or Most Expensive Liability)
(New York, Fireside, 2007)
http://blog.guykawasaki.com/2007/09/are-you-an-egom.html

[iv] John. F. Murray, Ph.D. "Losing With Style"
in column, Sports Psychology.
www.Tennis.com, official site of *Tennis Magazine*.

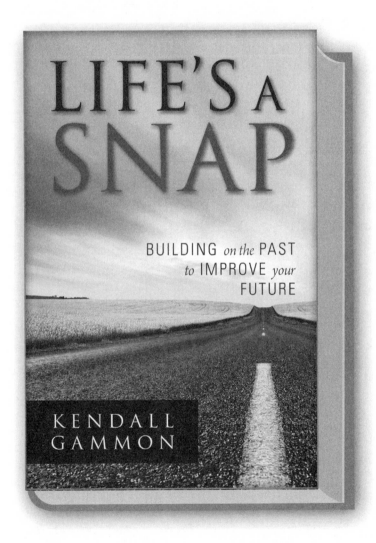